T0185090

Building Single Page Applications in .NET Core 3

Jumpstart Coding Using Blazor and C#

Michele Aponte

Apress®

Building Single Page Applications in .NET Core 3: Jumpstart Coding Using Blazor and C#

Michele Aponte
Torre del Greco (NA), Italy

ISBN-13 (pbk): 978-1-4842-5746-3   ISBN-13 (electronic): 978-1-4842-5747-0
https://doi.org/10.1007/978-1-4842-5747-0

Managing Director, Apress Media LLC: Welmoed Spahr
Acquisitions Editor: Joan Murray
Development Editor: Laura Berendons
Coordinating Editor: Jill Balzano

Cover image designed by Freepik (www.freepik.com)

Distributed to the book trade worldwide by Springer Science+Business Media New York, 233 Spring Street, 6th Floor, New York, NY 10013. Phone 1-800-SPRINGER, fax (201) 348-4505, e-mail orders-ny@springer-sbm.com, or visit www.springeronline.com. Apress Media, LLC is a California LLC, and the sole member (owner) is Springer Science + Business Media Finance Inc (SSBM Finance Inc). SSBM Finance Inc is a **Delaware** corporation.

For information on translations, please e-mail rights@apress.com, or visit www.apress.com/rights-permissions.

Apress titles may be purchased in bulk for academic, corporate, or promotional use. eBook versions and licenses are also available for most titles. For more information, reference our Print and eBook Bulk Sales web page at www.apress.com/bulk-sales.

Any source code or other supplementary material referenced by the author in this book is available to readers on GitHub via the book's product page, located at www.apress.com/9781484257463. For more detailed information, please visit www.apress.com/source-code.

Printed on acid-free paper

To my son, Francesco Paolo: I hope that one day you will read this book and be as proud of me as I am of you, especially every time you smile when you catch my eye.

Table of Contents

About the Author

Michele Aponte is a programmer who has worked with Java, .NET, and JavaScript at software and IT consulting companies in his native Italy since 1993. Combining his training, consulting, and development skills, in 2013 Michele founded Blexin to help customers migrate older software and systems to new technologies to improve their businesses. Passionate about programming, Michele embraces sharing with the community. He founded DotNetCampania, a Microsoft User Group in 2008, and has organized many regional conferences. He is also the founder of Blazor Developer Italiani, the Italian developer group about the Blazor framework. Recognized as a Microsoft MVP, he often presents on Microsoft and JavaScript topics at tech conferences throughout Italy.

Acknowledgments

Writing a book is hard work that requires a lot of time and inevitably involves the lives of those closest to the author. I want to thank my life partner, Raffaella, for her support for this project and her patience with me. I also want to thank my old friend, whose name is Raffaella as well, for the help she gave me in revising my English.

A special thanks also goes to all the employees of Blexin, my company, who are the best team one could have and with whom I can experiment every day with the technologies described in this book.

Finally, many thanks to the fantastic Apress team that supported me during this project.

Introduction

Blazor has garnered a great deal of enthusiasm since its initial release. I've followed the framework from the beginning, and when teaching any new technology, I use a practical approach. This book looks at the needs of real applications and answers all the questions you might have when learning how to use Blazor.

Specifically, in Chapter 1, I focus on the success of this framework and how it solves one of the problems most felt by Microsoft programmers: using JavaScript. Blazor allows you to use .NET directly in the browser, using open standards so as not to repeat the mistakes of the past. In my opinion, however, it is important to understand how Blazor works beyond the tools made available by the development environment, so I focus on the code in this book. I start with a simple example, without using the templates made available by Microsoft, to highlight how it works.

In Chapter 2, you will find a detailed comparison between the two versions of Blazor for web development: Blazor Server and Blazor WebAssembly. Using the example from the first chapter, I compare the two versions by highlighting what is going on behind the scenes and how WebAssembly is revolutionizing the world of front-end development. I explain how to choose a version based your requirements because they both have pros and cons and must be contextualized in your environment/situation.

In Chapter 3, I cover all the concepts necessary to create a single-page application, starting from scratch and tackling some issues concerning the decomposition of the interface into components. In this chapter, you will learn how to create pages and navigate between them, you will see how to create forms for data entry, and you will learn how to integrate the front end with the back-end, differentiating the approach between the two versions of the framework but standardizing their use thanks to the dependency injection of ASP.NET Core. Here you will discover that the framework allows you to invoke JavaScript functions from .NET and to invoke .NET methods from JavaScript functions.

In Chapter 4, I explain how to create libraries of reusable components, addressing how to generalize components thanks to the framework's ability to use .NET Generics and content projection. What may seem like more advanced aspects are actually necessary to avoid reinventing the wheel on each page of your application; this also allows you to start creating your own Blazor component library.

In Chapter 5, I cover application deployment, using both versions of the framework. It's important to know where your application will run, since scalability problems must be addressed and will impact how you write the application.

You can find the code for the first two chapters of the book in the `countdown` and `countdown-wasm` folders of the code download; you can use the two versions to see the differences between Blazor Server and Blazor WebAssembly within the same small application. The code for the third and fourth chapters, where you learn to create a small article manager, is available for both versions of the framework in eight pieces that follow the flow of the chapters.

- The application structure

- Pages and routing

- Components and their use in pages

- Back-end integration and shared library

- JavaScript interoperability

- Separation of the code into different files

- Blazor Library

- Custom input component

You can copy and execute the code that accompanies the book, but I suggest you write it from scratch by following the instructions in the chapters. That's the best way to learn Blazor!

CHAPTER 1

The Case for Blazor

During the Web 2.0 revolution, we had our first opportunity to port desktop applications to the Web. Thanks to the Ajax technology, which allowed us to do asynchronous calls to the server for the first time, we no longer had to suffer through a page reload every time the user updated the interface. We could finally get to the core of and resolve the main problems of desktop application development.

With a complete server-side application, we no longer need to install anything because we use the application through a browser, simplifying the release of the updates and controlling the current version used by our clients.

Unfortunately, all that glitters is not gold! If the user interface is entirely built on the server side, moving the application to the server has two distinct disadvantages. First, we must always be online to contact the server, and second, all the computational effort for the presentation layer passes from the customer's computer to the server.

To solve these problems, we need to move the user interface construction to the client. But if the application runs in a browser, we need to write a substantial part of the code in JavaScript, and if you are a .NET developer, this task has probably given you nightmares. If it has not, in this chapter we'll explore why it should with a simple example that would frighten anyone coming from a strongly typed language.

Microsoft provided developers with a solution to these problems via a front-end technology called Silverlight, together with a simplified

© Michele Aponte 2020
M. Aponte, *Building Single Page Applications in .NET Core 3*,
https://doi.org/10.1007/978-1-4842-5747-0_1

Windows Communication Foundation (WCF) back-end called Rich Internet Application (RIA) services, that allowed us to use the .NET Framework in the browser with the installation of a plug-in. Many companies invested in this technology, but a few years later, Microsoft decided to abandon the project, making those who today want to approach Blazor somewhat gun-shy.

But Blazor is different. Blazor is based on standard technologies, not Microsoft technologies. You don't need to install anything on your client, because the framework provides you with everything you need to use .NET Core in the browser, taking advantage of what is already there. If you are a Microsoft web developer and do not want to spend your time learning JavaScript frameworks, Blazor is the solution for you. I have helped many companies to adopt it successfully, and it has a low learning curve and allows you to reuse your .NET Core knowledge. In this chapter, we'll work to overcome your fear of JavaScript and get you on your way to creating your first Blazor application.

Why You Fear JavaScript

Why do I, as Microsoft developer, try to avoid JavaScript? Well, there are a few good reasons, but the driving one is the dynamic nature of the language with its runtime type checking and some other peculiarities that we will take a look at soon. Another important reason is the Microsoft approach to web development, which has always discouraged developers from using JavaScript.

With ASP.NET Web Forms, the approach was to drag and drop controls on the form, set their properties, and write code in event handlers. The Web Forms engine generated the HTML and JavaScript for you. Only with ASP.NET MVC do developers finally have control over their HTML and JavaScript, by using jQuery and its plugins for the main application development activities such as validation. It is also possible to use HTML helpers and data annotations with ASP.NET MVC to generate the correct configuration for the jQuery plugin (jQuery Unobtrusive Validation).

The jQuery library can help you with simple tasks such as DOM manipulation and asynchronous calls to the back-end, but moving the user interface construction onto the client means writing the entire front-end in JavaScript with all the problems of maintenance and productivity that the language can bring with it. Let's see why.

Code Nightmares

In all my JavaScript courses for .NET developers, I like to start the lessons by creating an example.js file and writing the code shown in Listing 1-1. This shows some JavaScript features that will surely impress a C# or Visual Basic developer and immediately clarifies the difficulties of a language so different from those .NET developers are used to using.

Listing 1-1. Some of the JavaScript Problems Summarized in a Single Script

```
function computes1() {
    a = 10;
}
function computes2() {
    a = 'hello'
}
computes1();
computes2();
console.log(a);
```

Without executing the code, what is the result? Are you scared? If you are not, you should be, because this code works, and the result is hello. That means the variable a cannot be declared anywhere, its scope is global, and its type can change without any problems from number to string. In the computes2 function, I omitted the semicolon because it is not required in JavaScript.

The language is case sensitive, so fullname and fullName are different variables. If you cannot declare a variable and you fail to write a variable name, the engine creates another global variable for you, with an incredible loss of time in your debug sessions.

Note   In JavaScript you can force the engine to check that variables are declared with the "use strict"; directive (I see the smiles of Visual Basic programmers), but it only comes in ECMAScript 5, so some old browser will ignore it.

If you are a competent programmer, you always declare your variables. In JavaScript you use the var keyword to do that, but let's look at the code of Listing 1-2. What's wrong?

Listing 1-2. Some JavaScript Peculiarity for a .NET Developer

```
function computes() {
    var a = 10;
    if(a == '10') {
        var b = 'ok';
    }
    console.log(b);
}
computes();
```

The execution result of the code is ok. Are you confused? The if statement is true because in JavaScript the == operator executes the type coercion between operands, converting the value of one operand to the type of another. If you convert the value of the variable a from the number

10 to the string '10', the result of the condition is true. If you do not want to allow this conversion, you can use the === operator.

The most interesting thing is that the b variable is declared in the if block, so you could imagine that console.log(b) returns an error both if condition is true and if it is false. Unfortunately, in JavaScript, the scope of a declared variable is always at the function level, not at the block level, so the b variable exists outside the if block.

Whether the if condition is false, which is the value of b? The assignment of the ok string will be not executed, so its value will be undefined. That is not null, but undefined, which is a possible value of a JavaScript variable that represents the state of declared but not initialized. I wish I could see your face right now!

Note   In ECMAScript 6 you can use the keyword let instead of var to declare a variable with block scope, but if your browser does not support it, an error will be generated.

Mitigate the Problem with TypeScript

Another problem with JavaScript is the adoption of the newest standard by browsers. For example, with ECMAScript 6 (ES6), we have class support, the let keyword, arrow functions, and some other improvements that can help to write more maintainable code, but some older browsers do not support ES6. This same problem will continue with the next versions, so we need a solution that permits us not to go crazy.

TypeScript is the response from Microsoft to this problem: it introduces a transpiler that translates the code written in a new language (TypeScript) to a target JavaScript standard.

> **Note**   I sometimes use *JavaScript standard* instead of the term ECMAScript because many developers do not know the history of JavaScript. If you are interested in exploring the history, take a few moments to learn about it from the legendary Douglas Crockford in his "Crockford on JavaScript" series. (If you don't know who he is, take a break to learn more: `https://www.youtube.com/watch?v=RO1Wnu-xKoY`.)

TypeScript is a superset of JavaScript that adds features to the language such as typing support and the ability to use all the constructs in any version of JavaScript, improving both the maintenance and the productivity of the application.

In short, you can write TypeScript code in a syntax that is similar to C#, with support for the current and next versions of JavaScript, and compile it (*transpile* is the correct term) in JavaScript code. In the end, it is always JavaScript, with all the limits that we have already talked about, but with TypeScript, you have a tool that checks the types of your variables and converts the code to a configured JavaScript standard while applying all the recommended best practices. (This conversion process is technically called *transpiling*, and the TypeScript compiler is called the *transpiler*.)

Why You Need a JavaScript Framework

TypeScript is a great help, and frameworks such as Angular and libraries such as React have adopted it to shorten the code refactoring process. However, think about writing your whole client with it: that would be like writing your application in C# without the .NET Framework. OK, maybe the comparison is a bit strong, but the concept is close to reality.

For this reason, frameworks like Angular were born. They offer you everything you need to build your client using JavaScript. Angular provides you with libraries to manage forms, to call a REST API back-end, to organize your application into a manageable structure, and to provide a dependency injection tool to improve testability and separation of concerns.

To improve the user experience, it is often necessary to create a single-page application to allow navigation within your application without actually navigating between physically separate pages. For this purpose, these frameworks provide a routing engine, which dynamically controls the navigation among different pages; the routing engine manipulates the DOM of your single page on the fly, while also updating the browser history.

The negative aspect of these solutions is their complexity, and in some cases the performance provided. Moreover, if you have some view models or data transfer objects (DTOs) provided by the API, you need to replicate them in TypeScript and keep them aligned. If your back-end changes, no compiler warns you that a change has happened, because you have two separate projects with two different technologies. Luckily, if your back-end is written in .NET Core, now you have Blazor, an attractive alternative!

You Can Have Your Cake and Eat It Too with Blazor

Microsoft released the release-to-manufacturing (RTM) version of Blazor with .NET Core 3, a new front-end framework that solves all the problems previously mentioned. Thanks to it, you can use C# and the .NET Core framework to write the front-end of your application, using all the technologies you already know if you are a Microsoft web developer.

You can use Razor, HTML, and C# to define the user interface and use anything you want for the rest of the application. Blazor lets you run the front-end directly in the browser, providing all the tools you need to create a single-page application.

Blazor was created in 2017 as a personal project of Steve Sanderson, who presented a preview of Blazor based on DotNetAnywhere, a .NET Intermediate Language (IL) interpreter, at NDC Oslo (`https://www.youtube.com/watch?v=MiLAE6HMr10&feature=youtu.be&t=31m45s`). After this presentation, Blazor was added to the ASP.NET GitHub repository as an experimental project, but the enthusiasm of the community convinced Microsoft to move the project to the ASP.NET team, replacing DotNetAnywhere with Mono, which is the most famous open source platform based on the .NET Framework (`https://www.mono-project.com/`).

With the .NET Core 3 release, Blazor has become part of the framework, with an ambitious roadmap. As you can see in Figure 1-1, at the moment you can create the front-end of a web application with Blazor, but the idea is to eventually be able to build desktop and mobile applications with it, going through a progressive web app (PWA) approach as an intermediate step.

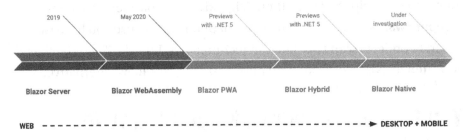

Figure 1-1. *Blazor roadmap*

Blazor Server is the version that ships with .NET Core 3, and it allows you to prerender the HTML of your application, execute the C# code on the server side, and push the user interface changes to the page through SignalR. Blazor WebAssembly is available from May 2020, and it executes the C# code directly in the browser. You can use Blazor WebAssembly with .NET Core 3.1.300 or later.

Blazor Hybrid will be a native .NET renderer to Electron and WebView, and it will be a native app that works online and offline. Electron (`electronjs.org`) is a popular open source project to create cross-platform desktop applications using web technologies. As an example, Visual Studio Code is based on Electron. Blazor Native, on the other hand, will have the same programming model but without HTML rendering. In this book, we talk about Blazor Server and Blazor WebAssembly because they are the only confirmed projects with precise dates of release, but Microsoft has long-term plans for this technology, so there's no time like the present to learn it.

Your First Blazor Application

"When it comes to new frameworks, I believe in a practical approach!"

Alastor Moody spoke of the dark arts in *Harry Potter and the Goblet of Fire*, and for me, it is the same. We will start with a simple application to get into the framework flow, and we'll use the minimum code that we need. Our first step will be to install all the necessary tools.

What You Need to Get Started

Blazor is based on .NET Core 3, but you can use your favorite operating system to follow the examples in this book (and on its GitHub repo). If you use Visual Studio, you are tied to Microsoft Windows. The development environment is important in a real development process, but for teaching purposes, I generally choose tools that are available for all operating systems supported by .NET Core.

The first step is to download and install .NET Core 3.1, from `https://dotnet.microsoft.com/download`. This release contains both Blazor Server, already available for production environments, and Blazor WebAssembly, which has been released in preview.

For a development environment, you can download Visual Studio Code, the free and cross-platform code editor from Microsoft. You can get it `https://code.visualstudio.com/`.

Getting Started

Now that we are set up with the right tools, we are ready to get started with our first Blazor application. We will use the .NET CLI, the command-line interface provided with .NET Core that allows us to create, build, and execute a .NET Core application. Microsoft provides some templates to start using Blazor, but I find it is educational to start from zero, both to learn how it is different from a classical .NET Core application and to learn how Blazor works. In our case, we need to create an empty web application. To do this, open the terminal window and execute the command `dotnet new web -o countdown`.

The .NET Core CLI creates the `countdown` folder, with all the starter code for a new application. Open the folder in Visual Studio Code to see the project structure. If you are already familiar with .NET Core, you will have noticed that this is the base structure of a web application (Figure 1-2).

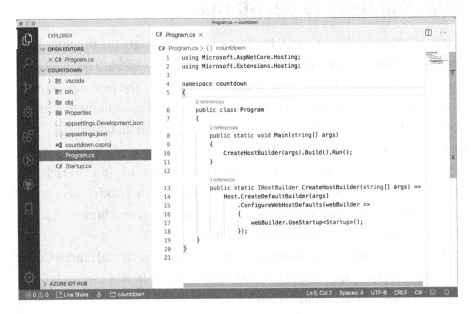

Figure 1-2. *Structure of a .NET Core 3.1 web project*

In Blazor Server, the server-side construction of the user interface is based on Razor Pages, an alternative approach provided by Microsoft to the MVC pattern. It is based on the concept of pages instead of controllers and views, and its goal is to be more productive and provide immediate results. In the Startup.cs file, we need to load the configuration for Razor Pages and Blazor Server, as shown in Listing 1-3.

Listing 1-3. Startup Configuration of a Blazor Server Application

```
public void ConfigureServices(IServiceCollection services)
{
    services.AddRazorPages();
    services.AddServerSideBlazor();
}
```

In the Configure() method, we need to add support for static files, the endpoints for the Blazor Server Hub, and the fallback for the page. Look at Listing 1-4.

Listing 1-4. Blazor Server Endpoints Configuration

```
public void Configure(IApplicationBuilder app,
IWebHostEnvironment env)
{
    app.UseStaticFiles();
    app.UseRouting();
    app.UseEndpoints(endpoints =>
    {
        endpoints.MapBlazorHub();
        endpoints.MapFallbackToPage("/_Host");
    });
}
```

The word Hub in endpoint.MapBlazorHub() should be familiar if
you already know how SignalR works, but we will go into more detail in
Chapter 2. The line endpoints.MapFallbackToPage("/_Host") sets the
page to navigate to if the specified resource is not found and also sets the
default page for our application. We need to create a file called _Host.
cshtml in a folder named Pages. The folder Pages is required by default,
because the Razor Pages engine searches for pages in this location.
The _Host.cshtml file contains the base HTML of the application and
the code for rendering our first Blazor component (Listing 1-5).

Listing 1-5. Blazor Server Host Page

```
@page "/"
@namespace countdown.Pages
<!DOCTYPE html>
<html lang="en">
<head>
    <title>Countdown App</title>
</head>
<body>
    @(await Html.RenderComponentAsync<Countdown>(
        RenderMode.ServerPrerendered))
    <script src="_framework/blazor.server.js">
    </script>
</body>
</html>
```

Blazor uses the same component concept as all modern UI
frameworks, in which a set of pieces, called Blazor *components*, composes
the user interface like in a puzzle. A Blazor component is, therefore, a
reusable piece of your user interface that can contain both HTML (with its
C# code) and other Blazor components.

I will talk about components in forthcoming chapters; for now, think of them as reusable pieces of your user interface. The RenderComponentAsync() method renders the component indicated in its generic parameter (Countdown in our case) with a server prerendered modality. This method of rendering a component is a peculiarity of Blazor Server and is not used, for example, in Blazor WebAssembly; we will talk about the differences in depth in Chapter 2.

The script _framework/blazor.server.js loads the JavaScript code of Blazor that permits the communication with the server. Note that to permit the loading of the script, we need to invoke the app.UseStaticFiles() method in the Startup class (see Listing 1-4).

It's time to create our first Blazor component! Let's create a file named Countdown.razor in the root folder. Our goal is to create a component that implements a simple countdown from 10 to 0 when the user clicks a Start button. Let's start with an intermediate step in which we define the user interface and initialize the countdown when someone clicks the Start button. See Listing 1-6.

Listing 1-6. Countdown Razor Component Start Code

```
@using Microsoft.AspNetCore.Components.Web

<h1>Countdown</h1>
<p>@count</p>
<button @onclick="startCountdown">Start</button>

@code {
    private int count = 0;
    private void startCountdown()
    {
        count = 10;
    }
}
```

The @page directive indicates the path where this component responds, and the using statement loads the elements of the Blazor framework. The markup defines your interface: a title, a paragraph, and a button. It is simple HTML with some Razor instructions. The @count instruction writes the value of the variable count. The framework updates the value in the paragraph for you when it changes. When the user clicks the Start button, the startCountdown() method is called thanks to the @onclick="startCountdown" statement.

The @code block allows you to define the C# code of the component. A Razor file is a C# class behind the scenes, so you can create attributes and methods to manage the status of your component. In Listing 1-6 we set the attribute count to the value 10 when the startCountdown() method is invoked. To implement a countdown, we need to add a timer that decreases the count to 0. Let's change the @code block as in Listing 1-7.

Listing 1-7. Countdown Razor Component Code

```
@code {
    private int count = 0;

    private void startCountdown()
    {
        count = 10;
        Timer timer = new Timer(1000);
        timer.Elapsed += (source, e) => {
            count--;
            if(count == 0) timer.Stop();
        };
        timer.Start();
    }
}
```

We created a simple Timer object that executes the callback subscribed to the Elapsed event every second (you need to add the instruction @using System.Timers at the top of the page to use the Timer class). It's simple, but it does not work because the code in the callback is executed in a separate thread, and when the variable count decreases, the change is not detected by the Blazor framework.

We can solve the problem by manually alerting the framework that the component state has been modified, calling the StateHasChanged() method. But this method must be invoked from the same thread of the user interface, and then we need to use the classical InvokeAsync() method. See Listing 1-8.

Listing 1-8. Countdown Razor Component Code Fixed

```
private void startCountdown()
{
    count = 10;
    Timer timer = new Timer(1000);
    timer.Elapsed += (source, e) => {
        count--;
        InvokeAsync(() => StateHasChanged());
        if(count == 0) timer.Stop();
    };
    timer.Start();
}
```

You can see the result in Figure 1-3.

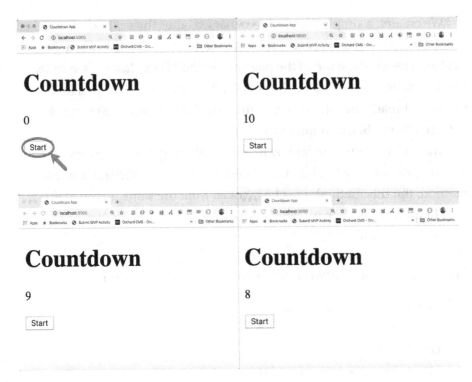

Figure 1-3. Our first Blazor Server app at work

Summary

In this first chapter, I talked about why Blazor is a viable solution for .NET developers who need to create a modern web application with a rich user interface without taking the time to learn the JavaScript language and frameworks.

You also learned that the first version of Blazor was released with .NET Core 3 and that a library ecosystem and complex use cases are not yet available but are forthcoming. In addition, you learned that Microsoft's vision for this technology is long-term, and the company is paying great attention to the use of web standards rather than proprietary technologies.

In the next chapter, I will cover how Blazor works internally and the main differences between Blazor Server and Blazor WebAssembly so you know which to pick for your needs.

CHAPTER 2

Blazor Server vs. Blazor WebAssembly

As I always say, there is not one tool that does everything but instead different tools for different requirements. A good programmer chooses his tools solely according to the requirements. You have to remember that requirements can be functional and nonfunctional, and often nonfunctional requirements are more important than functional ones for the success of an application.

You might think that Microsoft released Blazor Server before Blazor WebAssembly just because the latter was not ready yet; however, as you will see in this chapter, Blazor Server and Blazor WebAssembly solve the same problem with different approaches. You must choose which one will work best for you depending on your requirements.

How the Countdown Application Works

In Chapter 1, we created a sample application with Blazor Server that counts down from 10 to 0 when the user clicks a Start button. The code is simple if you know .NET, but how does it work behind the scenes?

Let's run the application and open it in your favorite browser. I use Google Chrome, but as you probably know, the new versions of Edge

© Michele Aponte 2020
M. Aponte, *Building Single Page Applications in .NET Core 3*,
https://doi.org/10.1007/978-1-4842-5747-0_2

use Chromium, the same engine as Chrome, so you can use Edge if you prefer it. Open the browser developer tools and go to the Network panel (Figure 2-1).

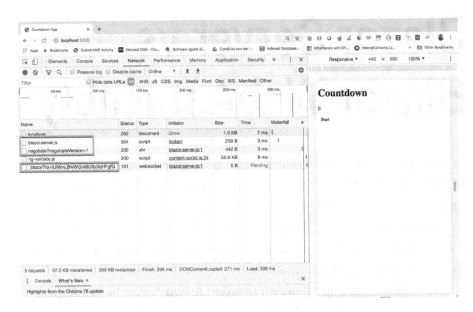

Figure 2-1. *Blazor Server application client downloads*

The HTML is rendered on the server side, and the script `blazor. server.js` is downloaded and executed in the browser. The script starts the connection with the SignalR Hubs API and opens a WebSocket from the server to the client.

SignalR is a Microsoft library that allows data to be pushed from the server to the client using the best-performing channel available. It is popular in the Microsoft ecosystem because it solves the problem of updating the client when something changes on the server, without having to rely on the classic JavaScript polling that periodically calls the server to check for changes to show in the interface. From the developer's point of view, it is sufficient to define a class that extends the base `Hub` class, from which it is possible to invoke a JavaScript callback in the client page. The library selects for you the best technique to implement the communication.

When the page loading is complete, the client library starts the negotiation with the server (the `negotiate?negotiatedVersion=1` call in Figure 2-1) to choose the best type of communication. If available, the first choice is the use of WebSocket, a standard protocol (RFC 6455, standardized for web browsers by the W3C) that provides a full-duplex communication channel over a single TCP communication. A WebSocket is the best choice in terms of performance but requires the support of both the browser and the application server. Usually, this is not a problem because all modern browsers support WebSocket, and looking at Microsoft solutions for web hosting, WebSocket is supported starting from Windows Server 2008 R2 and Windows 7; in addition, it is available on all the Windows Azure hosting services for web applications.

If the client and the server cannot start a WebSocket connection, the library downgrades to Server-Sent Events techniques. As with WebSocket, a Server-Sent Events communication pushes data from the server to the client without polling, but in this case, the communication is one way. After a first HTTP response of type `text/event-stream`, the server can send data that the client can receive with a simple callback on the `EventSource` object (Listing 2-1).

Listing 2-1. The JavaScript Callback to receive data in Server-Sent Events Communication

```
const eventSource = new EventSource('url');
eventSource.onmessage = (e) => {
  [...]
};
```

If Server-Sent Events is also unavailable, SignalR downgrades to *long polling* communication, an optimized variant of the type of polling where the client sends requests to the server to check for changes.

In the simple type of polling, if you send requests periodically, for example, every five seconds, you can have a five-second delay on the update, and if there are no changes, your requests consume resources without results. By contrast, long polling tries to mitigate these problems by leaving a request suspended and pending until a change occurs. When the client finally receives a response or the connection is lost for a network error, it immediately makes a new request.

Blazor Server uses SignalR to push the update of the user interface to the client. In Figure 2-1, you can see the opened WebSocket (_blazor?id= tUNimLBwWGmBUSy3qHFgfQ). If you click the WS tab of the Network panel, as in Figure 2-2, you can see the data exchanged in detail.

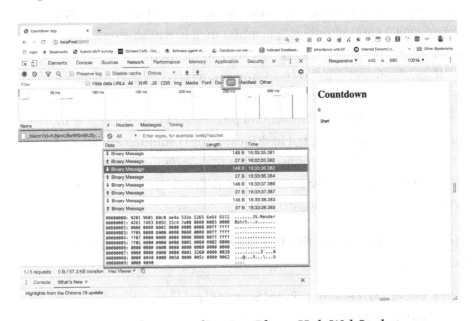

Figure 2-2. *Countdown application BlazorHub WebSocket*

As you can see in Figure 2-2, when the user clicks the button, a message is sent to the server (up arrow) that executes the request and sends to the browser the changes to be applied to the browser DOM (down arrow). The next messages are caused by the timer that every second updates the counter. The countdown timer is a server thread that updates the count variable (Listing 1-8), and when the Blazor engine detects a change, it updates the client interface through SignalR.

Note   Normally, the Blazor engine automatically detects the changes. In Listing 1-8 we had to explicitly call the StateHasChanged() method only because the change does not occur in the thread in which Blazor performs the change detection.

Running the Countdown Application in the Browser

With Blazor WebAssembly, all the application user interface code runs in the browser, without interaction with the server. You will call the server only if you need to use a web API to retrieve or save data, but the presentation will run on the client side. Let's see how it is possible.

To use Blazor WebAssembly, you only need to install .NET Core 3.1.300 or later. You can use a ready-to-run template by Microsoft without installing any templates, but if the system did not found them, you can run the command in Listing 2-2 and creating a sample project with the command dotnet new blazorwasm.

Listing 2-2. .NET CLI Blazor Project Template Installation Command

```
dotnet new -i Microsoft.AspNetCore.Components.WebAssembly.
Templates::3.2.0
```

However, to understand how the Blazor Server application is different from the WebAssembly version, I prefer to start from the same starting point used in Chapter 1 and then execute the command dotnet new web -o countdown-wasm. Open the `countdown.csproj` file to see the basic project configuration for a web application (Listing 2-3).

Listing 2-3. .NET Core Web Application Project File

```
<Project Sdk="Microsoft.NET.Sdk.Web">
  <PropertyGroup>
<TargetFramework>netcoreapp3.1</TargetFramework>
  </PropertyGroup>
</Project>
```

The first key concept you need to understand is that the result of a Blazor WebAssembly build is not a classic .NET web application. Instead, it is a set of files that the browser will download and execute locally. The web server, Kestrel in our case, is just a way to expose this set of files to the browser. The `countdown.csproj` file must be changed as shown in Listing 2-4.

Listing 2-4. .NET CLI Blazor Project Template Installation Command

```
<Project Sdk="Microsoft.NET.Sdk.Web">
  <PropertyGroup>
    <TargetFramework>netstandard2.1</TargetFramework>
    <RazorLangVersion>3.0</RazorLangVersion>
  </PropertyGroup>

  <ItemGroup>
    <PackageReference Include="Microsoft.AspNetCore.Components.
    WebAssembly" Version="3.2.0" />
    <PackageReference Include="Microsoft.AspNetCore.Components.
    WebAssembly.Build" Version="3.2.0" PrivateAssets="all" />
```

```
<PackageReference Include="Microsoft.AspNetCore.Components.
WebAssembly.DevServer" Version="3.2.0" PrivateAssets="all" />
  </ItemGroup>
</Project>
```

The first difference you have to note is the change of the
TargetFramework value in netstandard2.1; this allows the build of the
project with the correct dependencies. We also need to set the language
version for Razor (RazorLangVersion) to version 3.0 to allow the build of
Razor components. Finally, with the ItemGroup element, we declare all
the dependencies for the build and execution of the Blazor WebAssembly
engine.

Now open the Program.cs file and delete the static
CreateHostBuilder() method, because the framework provides us with a
simple API to start Kestrel directly in the Main method, like in Listing 2-5.

Listing 2-5. Blazor WebAssembly Host Builder

```
public static async Task Main(string[] args)
{
    var builder = WebAssemblyHostBuilder.CreateDefault(args);
    builder.RootComponents.Add<Countdown>("countdown");
    await builder.Build().RunAsync();
}
```

As you can see, you need only three rows of code to configure the
hosting of a WebAssembly application, create a WebAssemblyHostBuilder
with the default parameters, set the Countdown component as the Root
component, and start listening for HTTP requests in the application. You
do not need the Configure class, so you can delete it.

The file Countdown.razor is the same as the Blazor Server version, and you need to enter a copy in the root folder. However, we also need to render the Blazor component on the client side without the page _Host.cshtml.

To do this, we can add a wwwroot folder to the project and create an index.html file. The index file (Listing 2-6) is a classic HTML5 start page, but in the body block we use the Countdown component as an XML element. During page parsing, the browser ignores the <countdown> element because it is not a valid HTML5 element, but after loading the blazor.webassembly.js script, the Blazor component is recognized and executed.

Listing 2-6. The index.html File That Hosts Our Blazor Component

```
<!DOCTYPE html>
<html>
<head>
    <meta charset="utf-8" />
    <meta name="viewport" content="width=device-width" />
    <title>Countdown</title>
</head>
<body>
    <countdown>Loading...</countdown>
    <script src="_framework/blazor.webassembly.js"></script>
</body>
</html>
```

The Blazor component element is called countdown because in the Main() method we have specified the "countdown" string as a parameter for the RootComponent.Add<T>() method (Listing 2-4).

We are ready to run the application: execute the command `dotnet run` in the project folder and open the address `localhost:5000` in the browser with the Developer tools active on the Network tab (Figure 2-3).

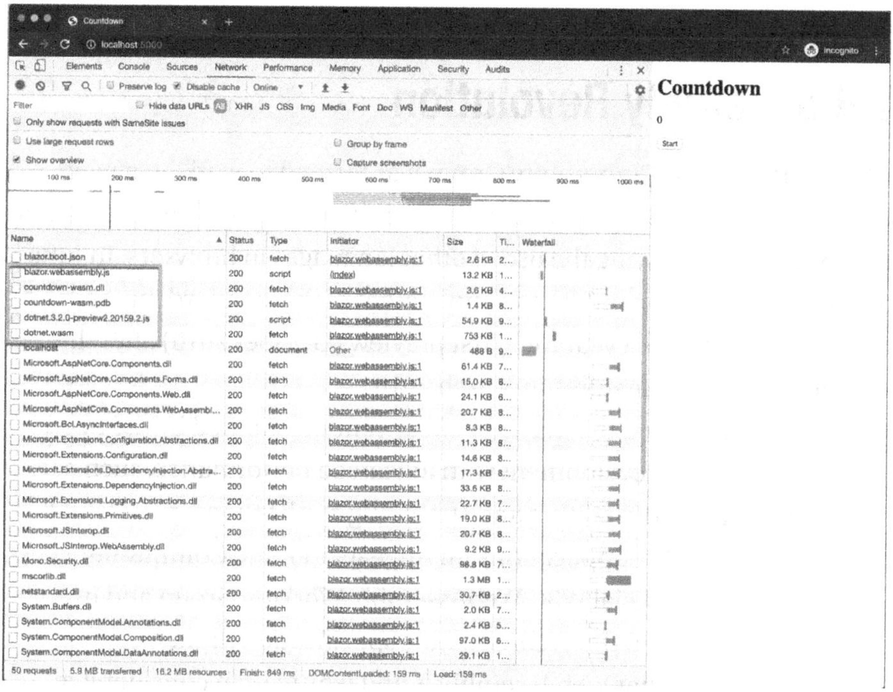

Figure 2-3. *Countdown Blazor WebAssembly application*

The first impact is really impressive, although seeing the DLLs downloaded in the browser can be confusing and bring up some bad memories (can you say Silverlight?). In this case, you have not installed any plug-in, so how does this work? The files highlighted in Figure 2-3 are the key. Thanks to them, the browser can execute the .NET code of the DLLs using the WebAssembly porting of the Mono framework. Specifically, the `countdown-wasm.dll` file contains our code compiled in Intermediate Language (IL) executed by Mono in the browser with the `dotnet.wasm` and `dotnet.js` files. The application uses various .NET DLLs also downloaded in the browser, including Blazor, that interact with the environment thanks to the `blazor.webassembly.js` script. All the DLLs libraries and the runtime components are cached in the browser, so they will not be downloaded in the next execution of the application.

WebAssembly Revolution

In April 2015, a W3C Community Group was formed to work on a new standard called WebAssembly, with the aim of overcoming the limitations of JavaScript and allowing the use of other languages in browsers. In June 2015 there was the first public announcement of the standard, but we had to wait more than a year for a first preview (October 2016) after the definition of the core features in March 2016.

The group included the major browser vendors, unified by the need to allow application development with advanced performance, such as games, video and audio editing and streaming applications, and virtual and augmented reality applications. In August 2017, the Community Group became the official W3C WebAssembly Working Group and in February 2018 released the WebAssembly specification draft.

To understand what WebAssembly is and why we can consider it a revolution in web development, let's clarify how JavaScript works in the browser. JavaScript code is interpreted in the browser by a sort of virtual machine called the JavaScript runtime, in which it can interact with the browser through specific APIs (the DOM, WebSocket, Web Storage, etc.). WebAssembly is placed in the same JavaScript runtime (Figure 2-4), which allows it to interact with the same browser APIs and even with JavaScript.

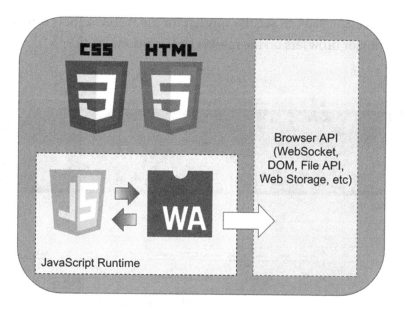

Figure 2-4. *JavaScript and WebAssembly in the browser*

The main difference is that the JavaScript code is interpreted by the JavaScript runtime, while the WebAssembly code is directly executed at near-native speed, since it is compiled in a WASM binary format that is close to the specification of the runtime. Furthermore, with the same code, the size of the compiled WASM code is obviously smaller than the corresponding JavaScript.

You can write WebAssembly code by yourself or use a high-level language like C++ or C # to generate the WASM code, but this new standard was designed to work with JavaScript, so you can call a JavaScript script from a WebAssembly function or invoke a WebAssembly function from a JavaScript script. This interaction can be useful in a hybrid scenario and is a powerful tool that offers you the best of both worlds.

You do not need to install any plug-in to use WebAssembly, because it is supported natively by the browser. Like all W3C standards, the support for WebAssembly is guaranteed in most of the latest browser versions (but not in all).

In Figure 2-5, you can see the support for the WebAssembly standard from the major browsers on the market (`www.caniuse.com`).

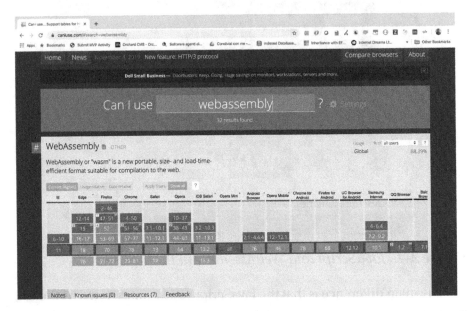

Figure 2-5. *WebAssembly browser support*

Which Blazor to Choose

The question now is, which version of Blazor is the best for your application? What criteria should you use when choosing between Blazor Server and Blazor WebAssembly?

When we compare loading time, Blazor Server is faster than WebAssembly because it runs on the server side, and therefore the download size is smaller. By contrast, a Blazor WebAssembly application runs completely in the browser, and it provides a full single-page application user experience against a heavier initial load.

If your application is completely executed on the client side, you can support an offline scenario, because it is not necessary to call the server for all user interface updates. On the other hand, if you have to store sensitive information, a server application allows you to store it more securely since the user does not have direct access to the data.

Finally, browser support for WebAssembly may be a reason to choose Blazor Server: there are still many applications that need to be run on Internet Explorer, for example, where the support for the new standard is not available.

Do we have to choose now? As you can see, only the configuration part of our application changed between Blazor Server and Blazor WebAssembly. There are other differences in a larger application, but you can control them using some design patterns, which allow you to switch from the server version to the WASM version with minimal impact. Read on to find out how.

Summary

In this chapter, we analyzed the main differences between Blazor Server and Blazor WebAssembly so you have all the information to choose the correct version of the framework based on your requirements. In the next chapter, we will get to the heart of the framework, discovering all the tools that Blazor provides so we can create a real single-page application using the .NET Framework and C#.

CHAPTER 3

Create Your Single-Page Application

Creating a single-page application is crucial if you want to develop an application with a well-performing and productive user experience. But it can be complicated and hard to maintain if you do not approach the development correctly.

Blazor can support you by providing all the necessary tools to create a successful application, as I describe in this chapter. Still, it is essential when designing your application to use the appropriate patterns and choose the correct tools in the right places.

Starting with the components, the core of all modern UI frameworks, you must learn how to separate functionalities and make them reusable. In a business application, where you collect data from the user, it is important to provide a good experience for data entry that includes validation and helps the user not to make errors.

In addition, to create a single-page application, you need a single page. The navigation between the pages takes place with the routing functionality that allows you to show a component based on user interaction or at the end of an operation. You also need to communicate with the back-end, using the HTTP protocol, and exchange information with the front-end. Last but not least, you must manage the security in your application, authenticating users and allowing them to do only certain operations.

© Michele Aponte 2020
M. Aponte, *Building Single Page Applications in .NET Core 3*,
https://doi.org/10.1007/978-1-4842-5747-0_3

Finally, you cannot forget to create code that is maintainable, testable, and straightforward. Using design patterns can help you, but they can solve only generic problems, and you still have to adapt them to your needs.

Everything Is a Component

Everything in your user interface is a component. In the previous chapters, you learned what a component is in Blazor, so now it is time to understand their importance.

A component is a piece of your user interface. Imagine a typical business application where you have a main menu, a footer, and the central area where you show a table of items (Figure 3-1). How many components do you see in it?

Main Menu					
My Items					
Show 10 ▼ entries .					Search:
Name	**Position**	**Office**	**Age**	**Start date**	**Salary**
Brielle Williamson	Integration Specialist	New York	61	2012/12/02	$372,000
Colleen Hurst	Javascript Developer	San Francisco	39	2009/09/15	$205,500
Garrett Winters	Accountant	Tokyo	63	2011/07/25	$170,750
Herrod Chandler	Sales Assistant	San Francisco	59	2012/08/06	$137,500
Rhona Davidson	Integration Specialist	Tokyo	55	2010/10/14	$327,900
Tiger Nixon	System Architect	Edinburgh	61	2011/04/25	$320,800
Showing 1 to 6 of 6 entries				Previous 1 Next	
Footer					

Figure 3-1. *Typical business application structure*

There are at least three main components: one for the main menu, one for the footer, and one for the table. Do you agree? This number is probably correct, but components in Blazor have a specific definition. A component must have the following characteristics:

- They can be contained, or they can contain other components.

- They can neither too big nor too small.

- They are reusable.

- They are customizable.

- They can be independent of other components.

- They must have logic.

Component Tree

From the structure of the components and their relationships, we must be able to create a tree of components with a root from which we extend the structure into leaves. Then we need a root component that contains our user interface. Blazor does not limit us to a single tree, and therefore to a single root container, but it is a good idea to manage our application from the point of view of the navigation.

Each component can contain other components, creating a parent-child relationship between them. Since we have to create a tree, a component cannot contain a child that is already its own parent. This would create a circular dependency, which would create a stack overflow, so it is not permitted.

Component Size

The size of a component depends on its purpose, but it is easy to get it wrong. Let's take as an example the main menu of the application, which can be a component. What about the menu items? We could create a component for a single menu item and use a set of them in the main menu component. If your menu item has an icon, should it be a component? We could continue like this down to a single character of each string in your interface.

Choosing the size of a component requires experience and a good knowledge of the domain, but you can use some general rules to start with. In software engineering, there is a rule called the *single responsibility principle*. It is directly connected to the separation of concerns and says that each element of a software system should perform only one task, which means it must have only one responsibility. When you think about your components, think about their responsibilities and create a component for each responsibility. Most of the time, this will be the right choice.

For example, take the list/details management aspect of an entity in your domain. Creating a component for the list management and one for the details management can be a good idea, but there may be cases where the simplicity of the data, like an entity with only one identifier and description, makes the use of two components an example of over-engineering. Context is king always.

Reusability, Customization, and Independence

Beyond the context, however, if you need to reuse a piece of the interface in different use cases, you can be sure that it is a component. Returning to the previous example, if there are other use cases in your application where you need the details form of an entity, it is surely a component separated from the list.

Imagine you have a list of articles and a list of article categories and you need to create a new article in which the category is not yet present in the list. To improve the user experience, you can show a button next to the category field in the article form and use it to create a new category on the fly and choose it for the article. In this case, you can reuse the details component of the category that is already used in managing the categories. Perhaps it would be better to show the component in a modal window instead of in the central area of the application. See Figure 3-2.

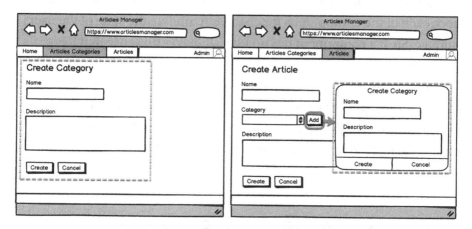

Figure 3-2. *Reusing a component in different use cases*

To allow this scenario, you need to make the component independent of its container and make it customizable. Modal forms generally have their owner title and buttons area, so it is necessary, for example, to check the visibility of the title and buttons to manage it differently in the two cases.

Being independent of the container also means controlling the behaviors of the user interaction with the component, which means, in the previous example, having the ability to do different actions when the user clicks the buttons. If you are in the article categories details form, after saving or clicking the Cancel button, you must return to the list of categories; therefore, in the modal form, you need to close the window and select the item created as a category for the current article.

Component Logic

Creating a component requires the generation of a class instance, which affects the performance of the application. Each component has its own state that requires memory space, and the Blazor framework must check each of the components for changes to update the state of the user interface. So, if a component has no logic, it makes no sense that it is a component.

For example, the footer component of our example probably contains only one string with the copyright information or the version of the application. You can show this information directly in the container component instead of its own component, simplifying the structure and saving resources.

Creating the Application Structure

Following the instructions provided in the previous chapters, we can create the basic structure of a single-page application project from scratch. You can apply all the concepts discussed in this chapter in both Blazor Server and Blazor WebAssembly, but we will use Blazor WebAssembly in this book; I will point out the differences from the Server version when relevant.

Suppose you want to create an article manager, a single-page application to manage the articles of a blog, and want to simplify the domain to manage only the articles and its categories. Let's start by creating a web application with the .NET CLI, calling it article-manager (dotnet new web -o article-manager-wasm), and referencing the needed packages, as illustrated in Chapter 2.

To simplify the layout, you can use version 4.3 of the Bootstrap CSS framework, referencing it by a CDN or downloading it into your project (https://getbootstrap.com/docs/4.3/getting-started/download/). If you prefer to have all the project dependencies offline, create a subfolder of the wwwroot folder named css and place in it the bootstrap.min.css file and an empty file named site.css, where you can place the custom CSS rules of the project.

While the project grows, it needs to import various namespaces that we can centralize for the Razor components in a file named _Imports.razor placed in the application's root folder. This allows us not to repeat them in each Razor file (Listing 3-1).

Listing 3-1. The _Imports.razor File Content, with All the Namespaces for the Project

```
@using System.Net.Http
@using Microsoft.AspNetCore.Components.Forms
@using Microsoft.AspNetCore.Components.Routing
@using Microsoft.AspNetCore.Components.Web
@using Microsoft.JSInterop
@using article_manager_wasm
```

We also need a container component, usually named App.razor, that for now will contain a welcome message (Listing 3-2).

Listing 3-2. The Container App.razor Component Code

```
<div class="container">
 <h2>Article Manager</h2>
 <p>Welcome to the article manager app.</p>
</div>
```

The single page index.html, placed in the wwwroot folder, references the CSS files and the app component, as shown in Listing 3-3.

Listing 3-3. The index.html File Content

```
<!DOCTYPE html>
<html>
 <head>
 <meta charset="utf-8" />
 <meta name="viewport" content="width=device-width" />
 <title>article-manager</title>
 <base href="/" />
 <link href="css/bootstrap.min.css" rel="stylesheet" />
 <link href="css/site.css" rel="stylesheet" />
 </head>
 <body>
 <app>Loading...</app>
 <script src="_framework/blazor.webassembly.js"></script>
 </body>
</html>
```

You can see the project structure for both Blazor Server and Blazor WebAssembly in Figure 3-3. The Blazor Server structure is slightly different, as described in Chapter 2. The most important difference is the index.html in the wwwroot folder on Blazor WebAssembly versus the corresponding _Host.cshtml file in the Pages folder on Blazor Server. In addition, for the Blazor WebAssembly project, I deleted the appsettings files, because we do not need any server-side configuration in this kind of project.

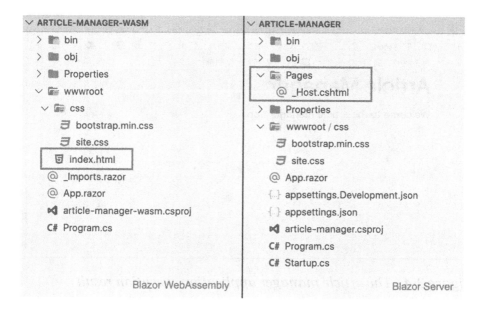

Figure 3-3. *Project structure for Blazor WebAssembly and Blazor Server*

In Figure 3-4, you can see the result of executing the project (dotnet run in the CLI or F5 in Visual Studio), which is the same for both Blazor Server and Blazor WebAssembly. The user result is the same, but with the WebAssembly version, all the code runs in the browser. By contrast, for the Blazor Server version, the back-end provides the HTML and keeps it updated via SignalR.

We are now ready to compose the application by creating the right components and hosting them, starting from the app container. To simplify this first attempt to use the components and to understand the role of the routing for the page navigation, we will not use the routing components yet; we will add them after learning how to structure the user interface from scratch.

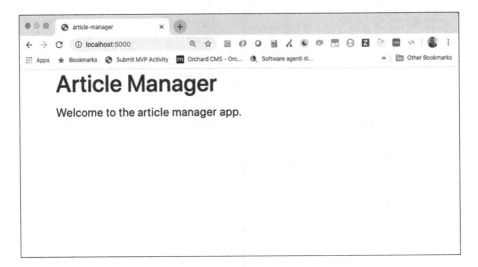

Figure 3-4. *The article manager application execution result*

The Main Menu Component

The main menu of the application is an excellent candidate to be a component: it contains a single functionality, its content depends on the context and current user, and it can be reused in various scenarios and applications. It is also a useful example to introduce the parametrization of a component because you can specify the menu items and capture the click on one of them.

Let's create a Shared folder in the project root, which we can use for all components shared with all sections of the application, and then create a file named MainMenu.razor containing the markup in Listing 3-4 and the code in Listing 3-5.

Listing 3-4. The Markup of the Main Menu Component

```
<nav class="navbar navbar-expand-sm bg-primary navbar-dark">
 <a class="navbar-brand" href="/">Article Manager</a>
 <ul class="navbar-nav">
```

```
@foreach (var item in MenuItems)
{
<li class="nav-item @(item.Active ? "active" : null)">
<a class="nav-link" href="#" @onclick="e => OnMenuItemClick.
InvokeAsync(item)">@item.Caption</a>
</li>
}
</ul>
</nav>
```

In this component, I use the navbar widget of bootstrap. The menu items are in a public property named MenuItems and decorated with the attribute [Parameter]. This attribute allows the container component to pass a value for the property, leaving Blazor to keep track of any changes.

Listing 3-5. The Code of the Main Menu component

```
@code {
 [Parameter]
 public EventCallback<MenuItem> OnMenuItemClick { get; set; }
 [Parameter]
 public MenuItem[] MenuItems { get; set; }
}
```

The property MenuItems is an array of a custom MenuItem class, which contains, for now, two properties: Caption, a string with the label of the menu item, and Active, a Boolean value that is true if the menu item is the current item and that is false otherwise (Listing 3-6). Usually, I place this kind of class in a folder named Models that represents the data model of the user interface.

Listing 3-6. The Code of the Main Menu Component

```
public class MenuItem
{
  public string Caption { get; set; }
  public bool Active { get; set; }
}
```

We are using the MenuItems array in a foreach loop and using the current element in the cycle to set the caption and the active class on the <li> element. If the user clicks the item, we capture this event (@onclick on the anchor element) and raise a custom event called OnMenuItemClick, passing the clicked item as an argument. OnMenuItemClick is another parameter of the MainMenu component, which is of type EventCallback<MenuItem>, an event handler delegate provided by the framework to simplify the definition of a custom event.

We are ready to use the MainMenu component in the App component, as shown in Listing 3-7 and Listing 3-8. All the public properties decorated with the attribute [Parameter] are visible on the MainMenu component, and we can use them directly in the markup (Listing 3-7). The App component and MainMenu components are in different folders, which means they have different namespaces. To allow the visibility of the MainMenu namespace to the App component, you need to add the namespace in the _Imports.razor file.

Listing 3-7. The Markup of the Main Menu Component in the App Component

```
<MainMenu MenuItems="MenuItems" OnMenuItemClick="MenuItemClick" />
<div class="container mt-3">
 <h2>Article Manager</h2>
 <p>Welcome to the article manager app.</p>
</div>
```

As an example, we have used an array of MenuItems initialized statically in a private method called loadMenuItems(). Here, there is a personal styling choice: I prefer to improve the code readability by using private and public methods that separate each operation in the components, but you are free to do this initialization inline with the declaration or the class constructor.

Regarding the constructor, a component provides you with many hooks to perform operations at various times of the component lifecycle. One of these is the OnInitialized method that you can override to do operations as soon as the component creation is complete. You can use it instead of the constructor to reduce the impact on the component creation time. It can be a useful optimization based on the complexity of the initialization operations, because if you place the same operations in the constructor, the component is created only at the end of them, with a delay of the user interface visualization. You can learn more about the component lifecycle hooks in the official documentation: https://docs.microsoft.com/en-US/aspnet/core/blazor/lifecycle?view=aspnetcore-3.1.

Listing 3-8. The Code That Manages the Main Menu Component in the App Component

```
@code {
 public MenuItem[] MenuItems { get; set; }
 protected override void OnInitialized()
 {
   this.loadMenuItems();
 }
 public void MenuItemClick(MenuItem item)
 {
   foreach (var menuItem in MenuItems)
   {
```

```
      menuItem.Active = false;
    }
    item.Active = true;
  }
  private void loadMenuItems() {
    this.MenuItems = new MenuItem[] {
    new MenuItem()
    { Caption = "Article Categories", Active = true },
    new MenuItem()
    { Caption = "Articles", Active = false }
    };
  }
}
```

Note the method MenuItemClick(), called when the OnMenuItemClick custom event is raised: the code sets the Active property of the MenuItems array to false and also sets the Active property of the item clicked to true. The change detection of Blazor notes this change and updates the user interface, setting the active class on the item clicked. The fascinating aspect is the way it executes the update: Blazor knows the state of the user interface, so when the code wants to change it, the framework computes the difference between the actual state and the new state and applies the difference only to the DOM of the browser. This technique, also used by many JavaScript frameworks, speeds up the update of the user interface significantly.

In Figure 3-5, you can see the result of our work. Using the OnMenuItemClick event, we can show or hide other components, simulating the page navigation. By doing it this way, besides being too laborious, we would also miss out on advanced navigation features, which we can get for free by using the routing features made available by the framework.

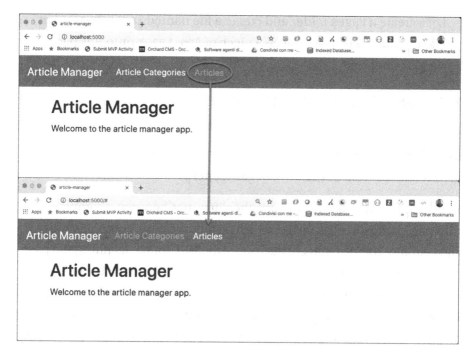

Figure 3-5. *The main menu component in action*

Page Navigation with Blazor

When creating a single-page application, the navigation between pages is crucial. Blazor provides specific components for this purpose that manage for us essential aspects of the routing, such as updating the browser history, managing a page not being found, and updating the URL.

To introduce Blazor routing, I need to highlight the difference between the components that are part of the page and the components that represent a specific page of the application. Usually, in a Blazor application, there is a folder called Pages that contains the components that are pages of the application; meanwhile, all the other components are in a Shared folders.

Let's create a Pages folder and create a file named Index.razor that represents your home page. Move a piece of App.razor onto this page, as shown in Listing 3-9.

Listing 3-9. The Home Page Component

```
@page "/"
<h2>Article Manager</h2>
<p>Welcome to the article manager app</p>
```

From a syntactical point of view, the difference between a component and a page is the directive @page, which creates the path/component pair, called a *route*. You can think of the root as the URL for navigating to the page.

Now you can add two more pages in the Pages folder, Article.razor and ArticleCategories.razor, with a simple title and the directive @page. You can use the code in Listing 3-10, where the first two rows are for the file Article.razor and the last two are for the file ArticleCategories.razor.

Listing 3-10. The Article Category and Articles Pages

```
@page "/articles"
<h2>Articles</h2>

@page "/articlecategories"
<h2>Article Categories</h2>
```

Now you have three pages, and it is time to decide in which area of your application you want to show a page when the user selects the corresponding route. In the Shared folder, create a MainLayout.razor component and put in it the code of Listing 3-11. MainLayout is not a page but a simple component that extends a base component of the framework, named LayoutComponentBase, that permits the router component to use it as a layout template. We can decide where the framework places the current page using the @Body placeholder, in the same way that you use it in the _Layout.cshtml file of a classical ASP.NET MVC application.

Listing 3-11. The Main Layout Component Markup

```
@inherits LayoutComponentBase
<MainMenu MenuItems="MenuItems" />
<div class="container mt-3">
  @Body
</div>
```

We need to change the MenuItem class to add the Href property and to indicate which path we can use for each menu item (Listing 3-12).

Listing 3-12. The Main Layout Component Code

```
@code {
  public MenuItem[] MenuItems { get; set; }
  protected override void OnInitialized()
  {
    this.loadMenuItems();
  }
  private void loadMenuItems() {
    this.MenuItems = new MenuItem[] {
    new MenuItem()
{ Caption = "Article Categories", Href = "articlecategories" },
    new MenuItem()
{ Caption = "Articles", Href = "articles" }
  };
  }
}
```

As you can see, you no longer need the custom click event, because the navigation and the active class management are responsibilities of the framework. MainMenu now only has the parameter MenuItems, which is the only thing you need.

You can use the framework's NavLink component in MainMenu
instead of the anchor. The main difference is the ability to use the Match
property. If you need to specify whether a menu item is the current one
(with the active class applied) when the route entirely matches the
current URL, you must use the value NavLinkMatch.All. If you need it to
match any prefix of the current URL, use the value NavLinkMatch.Prefix,
which is the default value. When using NavLink, you do not need the
property Active because the component sets the class on the generated
anchor automatically (Listing 3-13). Your App.razor component now
must contain the Router component, like in Listing 3-14, so when the
application starts, the router can control the application navigation.

Listing 3-13. The MainMenu with the NavLink component

```
Article Manager
 @foreach (var item in MenuItems)
 {
 @item.Caption
 }
```

Listing 3-14. The New App Component with the Router Component
Markup

```
<Router AppAssembly="@typeof(Program).Assembly">
 <Found Context="routeData">
 <RouteView RouteData="@routeData" DefaultLayout=
 "@typeof(MainLayout)" />
 </Found>
 <NotFound>
 <LayoutView Layout="@typeof(MainLayout)">
 <p>Sorry, there's nothing at this address.</p>
 </LayoutView>
 </NotFound>
</Router>
```

The router inspects the current assembly (`AppAssembly` parameter) to retrieve all the routes defined in the application using the `@page` directive.

If the router finds the requested route (`Found` element), it shows the page passing the route data and the default layout (the `MainLayout` defined previously); otherwise, it shows the layout with a message (`NotFound` element). If you have experience using JavaScript frameworks, you will appreciate this approach very much; the routing configuration is usually more complicated. In Figure 3-6, you can see the results of the refactoring, which include updating the URLs, updating the browser history, and activating the correct menu item to navigate between the pages.

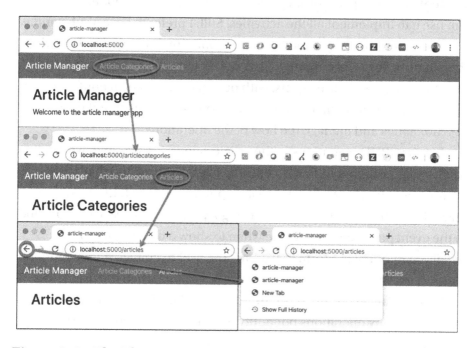

Figure 3-6. *The Blazor routing in action*

Managing CRUD Operations

The base structure is ready, so it is time to implement the application functionalities, such as the create, read, update, delete (CRUD) operations, on the article categories. We can generalize the activities, but for now, we'll focus on the separation of concerns, particularly on the Blazor components' responsibilities.

We need to show the list of categories and allow the user to add, modify, or delete a single item. Based on the requirements, we could have one component for the list and one for the details, or we could have one element for both operations. We already have a page component, so we can use it to implement all the activities. Still, I prefer to have a substantial difference between pages and UI components, implemented by following this simple rule: a UI component accepts input parameters to obtain the data to manage and raise events, with output parameters to notify the actions. A page, instead, uses the UI components to implement page functionalities and manage the flow of the operations.

For the CRUD operations in the article categories, we can have a category list component that accepts the items to show and that raises events when the user clicks the create, update, or delete button. We can place this component in the article category page, where we can subscribe to the event parameters to decide when to show a details component. A details component is a form that allows the user to change the category data, accepts an input parameter, and raises events when the user clicks the Save or Cancel button. It is important that the UI components do not perform any operations but notify the page component of the user intentions.

Let's change the previously created `ArticleCategories.razor` to match Listing 3-15. You can see the two UI components, placed in a folder called `Components`, managing the list and the details for the article categories with their parameters. We show the list component

if an attribute currentCategory is null; otherwise, we show the
ArticleCategory component that represents the category details.

Listing 3-15. The Article Categories Page Component

```
@page "/articlecategories"
<h2>Article Categories</h2>
<div class="mt-3">
@if(currentCategory == null)
{
 <ArticleCategoriesList
 ArticleCategoryListItems="articleCategoryListItems"
 OnAddClick="AddCategory"
 OnEditClick="EditCategory"
 OnDeleteClick="DeleteCategory">
 </ArticleCategoriesList>
}
else
{
 <ArticleCategory
 Category="currentCategory"
 OnSaveClick="SaveCategory"
 OnCancelClick="ShowList">
 </ArticleCategory>
}
</div>
```

The ArticleCategoriesList component is a simple table created with
a foreach loop on the parameter ArticleCategoryListItems, like the
MainMenu, with three buttons connected to the OnAddClick, OnEditClick,
and OnDeleteClick events (Listing 3-16). Basing on these events, the
code sets a value for the currentCategory attribute to manage the
ArticleCategory component's visibility.

Listing 3-16. The Article Categories List Component

```
<button class="btn btn-primary" @onclick="OnAddClick">Add
Category</button>
<table class="table mt-3">
  <thead>
    <tr>
      <th></th><th>Id</th><th>Name</th><th></th>
    </tr>
  </thead>
  <tbody>
  @foreach(var item in ArticleCategoryListItems)
  {
    <tr>
      <td>
        <button class="btn btn-warning" @onclick="e =>
        OnEditClick.InvokeAsync(item)"> Edit</button>
      </td>
      <td>@item.Id</td>
      <td>@item.Name</td>
      <td>
        <button class="btn btn-danger" @onclick="e =>
        OnDeleteClick.InvokeAsync(item)"> Delete</button>
      </td>
    </tr>
  }
  </tbody>
</table>
```

Creating a CRUD Service

Before describing how to implement these operations, we need to talk about the single responsibility principle again. In this case, we do not want to implement the data CRUD operations physically in the page component. To understand the reason, you can move the data operations somewhere else, remembering that a component is a piece of the user interface and that a page is also a component.

The physical CRUD operations belong to the business layer, and we are on the presentation layer. In our case, this distinction is crucial, because if we use Blazor WebAssembly, we need to call an API to require the operations, but if we use Blazor Server, we can have direct access to the database context to execute the CRUD operations. The component must not know anything about this, so we need to encapsulate the operation invocation in a separate service class. We can abstract the operations with a generic interface, like in Listing 3-17, using T for the list item type and K for the detail item type. We should design the operation to be asynchronous, using the .NET Task libraries (include the System. Threading.Tasks namespace) to be sure that the operations do not lock the current thread.

Listing 3-17. The CRUD Definition Interface

```
using System.Threading.Tasks;
public interface ICRUDService<T, K>
{
  Task<T[]> GetList();
  Task<K> Get(int id);
  Task Create(K item);
  Task Update(K item);
  Task Delete(int id);
}
```

You could have more implementations of this interface. For example, you could have an implementation based on the HTTP client that calls the corresponding REST APIs or an implementation that uses the entity framework database context for the Blazor Server version of the application. For testing purposes, you could also have an implementation that uses an in-memory collection, by registering the correct implementation for your case and using the native .NET Core dependency injection support in the ConfigureServices() method of the .NET Core Startup class (Listing 3-18).

Listing 3-18. The CRUD Service Configuration for Article Categories

```
public void ConfigureServices(IServiceCollection services)
{
    services.AddTransient <ICRUDService<ArticleCategoryListItem,
    ArticleCategoryItem>, ArticleCategoriesService>();
}
```

You can use the registered implementation of the service directly in the Blazor component, thanks to the new @inject directive introduced with .NET Core. In the article categories page, you can add the @inject instruction shown in Listing 3-19, where you specify the interface with the correct parameter for your case.

Listing 3-19. The CRUD Service Injection in the Page Component

```
@page "/articlecategories"
@inject ICRUDService<ArticleCategoryListItem,
ArticleCategoryItem> service
```

ArticleCategoryListItem and ArticleCategoryItem, placed in the Model folder, define the data used in the list (Id and Name) and the detail form (Id, Name, and Description). The ArticleCategoryItem class shows a powerful way to implement the data validation, already known by .NET programmers: .NET data annotations (Listing 3-20).

Listing 3-20. The Validation Rules Definition with .NET Data Annotations

```
using System.ComponentModel.DataAnnotations;
public class ArticleCategoryItem
{
  public int Id { get; set; }
  [Required]
  [StringLength(50, ErrorMessage = "Name is too long.")]
  public string Name { get; set; }
  public string Description { get; set; }
}
```

Yes, you can use .NET data annotations with the Blazor framework to implement form validation. Let's see them in action by creating the component ArticleCategory.razor in the Components folder to manage the form details. In Listing 3-21, you can see the markup of this new component that uses specific Blazor components to simplify the management of a form.

Listing 3-21. The Validation Rules Definition with .NET Data Annotations

```
<EditForm Model="@Category" OnValidSubmit="@(e => OnSaveClick.
InvokeAsync(Category))">
 <DataAnnotationsValidator />
 <ValidationSummary />
 <div class="form-group">
 <label for="name">Name: </label>
```

```
<InputText id="name" @bind-Value="Category.Name" class="form-
control" />
<ValidationMessage For="@(() => Category.Name)" />
</div>
<div class="form-group">
<label for="description">Description: </label>
<InputTextArea id="description" @bind-Value="Category.
Description" class="form-control" />
</div>
<button type="submit" class="btn btn-primary">Save</button>
<button type="button" class="btn btn-warning"
@onclick="OnCancelClick">Cancel</button>
</EditForm>
```

In Blazor, you can define a form in the EditForm component element, for which you can set a model and subscribe to an event raised when the user submits the form. If you subscribe to the OnValidSubmit event, your code runs only when the form is valid, and the validation follows the rules of the .NET data annotations of the specified model. To enable model validation based on data annotations, you need to include the component DataAnnotationsValidator in the form. The framework provides you with the ValidationSummary component to show a summary of the failed validations, along with the ValidationMessage component to show the validation error of a specific field. The framework provides specific components to help you show the correct input element and bind it with the corresponding Model property using @bind-Value.

Let's see how to manage the events of the components in the article categories pages. In Listing 3-22, you can see an extract of the code that manages the currentCategory attribute.

Listing 3-22. The Code of the Article Categories Page

```
protected override async Task OnInitializedAsync()
{
  await ShowList();
}
public async Task ShowList()
{
  this.articleCategoryListItems = await service.GetList();
  this.currentCategory = null;
}
public void AddCategory()
{
  this.currentCategory = new ArticleCategoryItem();
}
public async Task EditCategory(ArticleCategoryListItem item)
{
  this.currentCategory = await service.Get(item.Id);
}
```

The ShowList() method calls the service to obtain the list of categories and set the currentCategory to null to show the list. The service methods are asynchronous, so we need to use the async/await keywords and the asynchronous version of the OnInitialized component hook.

When the user clicks the Add Category button or the Edit button, we set the currentCategory attribute to a new object or to the requested item to edit. In the solution provided with the book, you will find the rest of the code that manages the save and delete events using a try { ... } catch { ... } block to show a possible error to the user. In Figure 3-7, you can see the user interface in action.

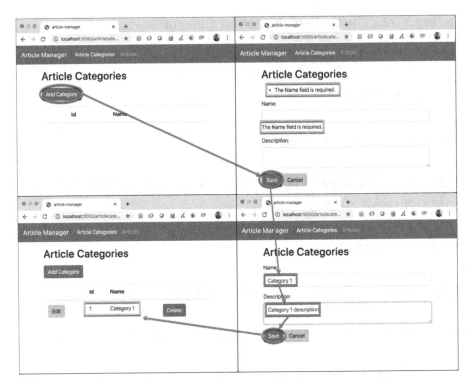

Figure 3-7. *The article category CRUD in action*

If you already know Microsoft web frameworks, all this information will seem familiar to you. This is the real power of Blazor for .NET developers.

Implementing CRUD Services

For testing purposes, I have created an in-memory implementation of the CRUD services. In a real application, you would need to store information in persistent storage, like a database. If you use Blazor Server, this is an effortless task, because you can inject the Entity Framework data context (or your preferred data access layer solution) in the CRUD service implementation and use it to execute all the operations.

If you use Blazor WebAssembly, you need to call REST APIs to allow the client to request the data storage. In this case, we have to create a CRUD service implementation that uses HttpClient (Listing 3-23).

Listing 3-23. The Code of the CRUD Service That Uses the HttpClient

```
using System.Net.Http.Json;
using System.Net.Http;
public class ArticleCategoriesService:
  ICRUDService<ArticleCategoryListItem,
    ArticleCategoryItem>
{
  private readonly HttpClient httpClient;
  private string baseUrl = "http://localhost:5002";

  public ArticleCategoriesService(HttpClient httpClient)
  {
    this.httpClient = httpClient;
  }

  public Task<ArticleCategoryListItem[]> GetList()
  {
    return this.httpClient
    .GetFromJsonAsync<ArticleCategoryListItem[]>
      ($"{baseUrl}/api/articlecategories");
  }
  ...
}
```

To use HttpClient, we must add the System.Net.Http.Json NuGet packages to our solution and add the System.Net.Http namespace to our CRUD service implementation. The Blazor framework provides some HttpClient extensions (the HttpClientJsonExtensions class in the System.Net.Http.Json namespace) that help to send and receive .NET classes, converting them to JSON format. In Listing 3-23, we can see GetFromJsonAsync, which receives from the API the JSON array of the article categories and converts it to a .NET array of ArticleCategoryListItem.

We also need to add HttpClient manually to the services because it is no longer added for you by the framework. Then, in the Main method of the Program class, use the AddTransient() method (Listing 3-24) to properly configure the HTTP client.

Listing 3-24. The Configuration of the HttpClient as a Dependency Service

```
public static async Task Main(string[] args)
{
    var builder = WebAssemblyHostBuilder.CreateDefault(args);
    builder.RootComponents.Add<App>("app");
    builder.Services.AddTransient <ICRUDService<ArticleCategoryL
    istItem, ArticleCategoryItem>, ArticleCategoriesService>();
    builder.Services.AddTransient <ICRUDService<ArticleListItem,
    ArticleItem>, ArticlesService>();
    builder.Services.AddTransient<HttpClient>();
        await builder.Build().RunAsync();
}
```

If we move the Model classes in a separate DLL and share this library with both the back-end and the front-end, the ASP.NET Core API on the back-end and the HTTP Client on the front-end will execute all the work for us, using JSON as the exchange format.

I suppose you already know how to save an entity with Entity Framework and how to create an API REST with .NET Core. In Listing 3-25, you can see the corresponding code of the API, but you can find the complete codebase used in these examples in the code provided with the book.

Listing 3-25. The Code of the ASP.NET Core API Used in Listing 3-23

```
[ApiController]
[Route("api/[controller]")]
public class ArticleCategoriesController :
  ControllerBase
{
    private readonly ApplicationDbContext db;

    public ArticleCategoriesController(
      ApplicationDbContext db)
    { this.db = db; }

    [HttpGet]
    public IActionResult Get()
    {
      return Ok(this.db.ArticleCategories
        .Select(x => new ArticleCategoryListItem()
        {
          Id = x.Id, Name = x.Name
        }).ToList());
    }
    ...
}
```

The impressive aspect is that the components are agnostic about these implementations. We need only to register the correct version of the CRUD service in the .NET Core dependency injection engine.

Where to Place the Component Code

So far, we have seen the component code in the Razor file, using the @code section. For small components, like our components here, this can be a useful solution, but if you have enough code to handle and want to keep the system separate from the markup, you can place the component code in a different C# class.

For example, if you want to separate the code of the ArticleCategories page component from its markup, you have two ways to do this. The first way is to create a base class file with a name different from the page name, but I advise you to use a convention that retains the link between them. We can use, for example, ArticleCategoriesBase.cs, which contains a class named ArticleCategoriesBase that extends the framework class ComponentBase (Listing 3-26).

Listing 3-26. The Class Containing the Article Categories Code

```
using Microsoft.AspNetCore.Components
public class ArticleCategoriesBase : ComponentBase
{
  ...
}
```

This class is now our base class for the Razor component, thanks to the @inherits directive (Listing 3-27).

Listing 3-27. The Component Markup Change to Inherit the Code Class

```
@inherits ArticleCategoriesBase
@page "/articlecategories"
```

Now we can move the content of the @code section in the ArticleCategoriesBase class, with only two changes: the private properties must be protected, and the injection of the CRUD service happens with the Inject attribute on a specific property (Listing 3-28).

Listing 3-28. The Changes You Must Apply to the Code When Moving It into a Separate Class

```
public class ArticleCategoriesBase : ComponentBase
{
  protected ArticleCategoryListItem[] articleCategoryListItems;
  protected ArticleCategoryItem currentCategory;

  [Inject]
  private ICRUDService<ArticleCategoryListItem,
  ArticleCategoryItem> service { get; set; }
  ...
}
```

Note   You cannot use the constructor to inject dependencies in a ComponentBase because the framework constructs the components for you. At the moment, the framework needs a constructor without parameters, so it provides the Inject attribute to solve the problem.

Another way to separate the code and markup of the component is to create a partial class. If you explore the obj folder generated during the build process, you will find a class for each component of your application. This class, generated by the compiler, is a partial class, so another partial class can be placed next to it. You can try this option with the Articles page, remembering that all the partial classes in the .NET Framework must have the same name (Listing 3-29) and you do not need to modify the visibility of the attributes used (at build time, partial classes with the same name become the same class). When you use a partial class to separate the code from the markup, it is common to name the file with the same name of the page, adding the `.cs` extension at the end. In this case, the file is named `Article.razor.cs`. Visual Studio uses this convention to show this file as a child of the page, grouping the two files as the same element. Visual Studio Code, instead, is not so smart.

Listing 3-29. The Class That Contains the Articles Code

```
public partial class Articles
{
    private ArticleListItem[] articleListItems = new
    ArticleListItem[0];
    private ArticleItem currentArticle;
    private string error;
    [Inject]
    private ICRUDService<ArticleListItem, ArticleItem> service {
    get; set; }
}
```

In this case, you must add only the code for the injection of the CRUD services and remove the `@inject` directive from the markup file.

JavaScript Interoperability

Until there is a complete ecosystem that supports all the possible functionality for an application, sooner or later you will need to invoke a JavaScript function. You will probably also need to invoke a .NET function from JavaScript. These scenarios are both supported in Blazor and resolve all the main problems with legacy code integration for your application.

To call a JavaScript function from Blazor, we must define it on the browser window object. Adding the jQuery and Bootstrap JavaScript libraries to the project, you can create a js folder in wwwroot and add the references in the file. These libraries allow us to use the bootstrap widgets, such as the Modal component (see the official documentation at https://getbootstrap.com/docs/4.0/components/modal/).

Let's add two JavaScript functions to the browser window object that open and hide a bootstrap modal, as shown in Listing 3-30. To simplify the example, I placed them in the index.html file, but in a real project you could place the JavaScript functions in a separate file and link to it.

Listing 3-30. JavaScript Functions to Show and Hide a Bootstrap Modal

```
<script src="js/jquery.min.js"></script>
<script src="js/bootstrap.min.js"></script>
<script>
  window.showConfirmDelete = (id) => {
    $('#' + id).modal('show');
  };
  window.hideConfirmDelete = (id) => {
    $('#' + id).modal('hide');
  };
</script>
```

Add the markup of a modal to the ArticleCategoriesList component, and set the modal to require the delete confirmation from the user (Listing 3-31).

Listing 3-31. Bootstrap Modal to Require Category Deletion

```
<div class="modal" id="deletecategorymodal">
 <div class="modal-dialog">
  <div class="modal-content">
   <div class="modal-header">
    <h4 class="modal-title">Delete Category</h4>
    <button type="button" class="close" data-
    dismiss="modal">&times;</button>
   </div>
   <div class="modal-body">
    Do you want to delete the category?
   </div>
   <div class="modal-footer">
    <button type="button" class="btn btn-danger"
    @onclick="OnYesClick">Yes</button>
    <button type="button" class="btn btn-default"
    data-dismiss="modal" >No</button>
   </div>
  </div>
 </div>
</div>
```

To call the JavaScript functions previously defined, you need to inject the framework's IJSRuntime interface in the component. You can do this by adding the directive @inject IJSRuntime JSRuntime at the top of the component definition. See Listing 3-32.

Listing 3-32. The Component Code That Calls the JavaScript
Functions

```
private ArticleCategoryListItem itemToDelete;
private async Task ShowConfirm(ArticleCategoryListItem item)
{
    this.itemToDelete = item;
    await JSRuntime.InvokeVoidAsync ("showConfirmDelete",
    "deletecategorymodal");
}
  private async Task OnYesClick()
  {
      await OnDeleteClick.InvokeAsync (this.itemToDelete);
      await JSRuntime.InvokeVoidAsync ("hideConfirmDelete",
      "deletecategorymodal");
  }
```

The JSRuntime provides the method InvokeVoidAsync that we can use
to call the JavaScript function and pass it the right parameters.

If the user clicks the Yes button, we invoke the event to require the
category deletion and invoke the hideConfirmDelete JavaScript function.
In Figure 3-8, you can see the confirmation modal in action.

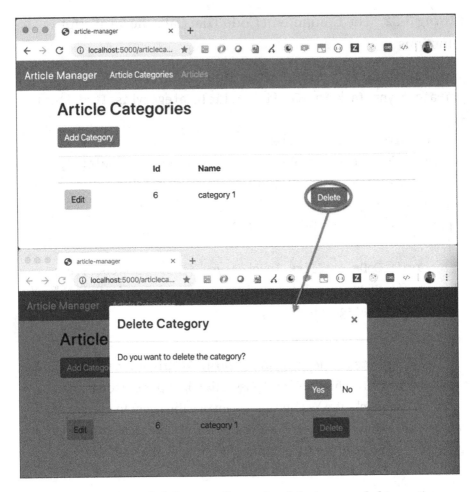

Figure 3-8. *The modal that confirms the deletion modal in action*

Summary

In this chapter, you learned how to build a single-page application with Blazor to perform CRUD operations on business entities. You saw how to generalize the code, using the .NET Core dependency injection to quickly adapt everything to be used with both Blazor WebAssembly and Blazor

Server. You also learned how to integrate JavaScript into Blazor, how to manage legacy scenarios, and how to take advantage of features that are not yet available in Blazor.

Much of the code in this chapter was deliberately repetitive, and some implementations are a little crude for educational reasons. Still, in the next chapter, you will see how to optimize the code, making the components even more generic, so that they can also be reused in different applications by packaging them in libraries of components.

CHAPTER 4

Build Your Reusable Blazor Library

Some components will be specific to your application, and others will not be. Think about the table of two CRUD operations that you created for the article-manager application in the previous chapter, or a Bootstrap modal for your front-end; also, some form component can be specific or not, such as an advanced select control or date picker.

In this chapter, I show you how to extract components from the project to a reusable library so you can potentially use them in different projects. Following this approach, your next project will start from a collection of your own ready-to-use component libraries.

You can extract a component from a project to put it in a library, or you can create a component directly in a library and use it in a project. In the first case, you probably need to generalize the component; in the second case, you need to design it outside of the specific use, profiting from the parametrization and principles learned in the previous chapter. You can also choose to create a component library to simplify the front-end. In a large project, this helps you to divide the job among different members of a team and to create a more maintainable project structure.

Many large companies and independent developers are creating generic components to add to the Blazor ecosystem. You can choose their libraries, creating a dependency on them, or you can create your own

© Michele Aponte 2020
M. Aponte, *Building Single Page Applications in .NET Core 3*,
https://doi.org/10.1007/978-1-4842-5747-0_4

libraries. There are pros and cons in both cases, but if you know how to build a library, then you can decide whether to create one or pick a ready-made one.

While extracting a component from a library, you will see some advanced features of the Blazor framework that are available for both the Server and WebAssembly version. Some of these features are useful but could complicate your codebase. The rule is always the same: follow the single responsibility principle and try to create value for your project and customer.

Creating a Component Library

The first step is to create a component library. The .NET CLI provides a template to create a Razor class library, which is perfect for us: launch the command dotnet new razorclasslib -o frontendlib in the root folder of the article-manager project. The -o option specifies the output of the command and creates a folder named frontendlib with the project inside it. Now we can go inside the frontendlib folder and add the library to the project with the dotnet add reference ../frontendlib command.

The razorclasslib template creates a sample component, with an example of the JavaScript interoperability with Blazor, and a wwwroot folder that contains static files. You do not need these files, so delete all of them except for the wwwroot folder and the _Imports.razor file.

Let's begin with the List component to generalize the entity list visualization. Our goal is to reuse the interface that lists one entity (for example, the article category) for each entity of your application. If you analyze the code of ArticleCategoryList, you can see that there is a simple HTML table with a fixed-column definition and a loop on an array of ArticleCategoryListItem. For the columns, you could use a parameter like a simple array of strings that contains the column headers; for the array, you can use a .NET object or a .NET generic. Let's start with a .NET object.

Create two folders, Components and Models, to contain the component files and the model classes to support them. In the Models folder, create a class to collect all the parameters for the List component, which simplifies the use of the component and its evolution with the creation of a unique parameter. In Listing 4-1, you can see an example of this class, named ItemListModel, that contains a string with the name of the entity, a collection of headers, and an array of objects.

Listing 4-1. The List Component Model Class Definition

```
public class ItemListModel
{
  public string ItemName { get; set; }
  public string[] Headers { get; set; }
  public object[] Items { get; set; }
}
```

At this point, you can create a new component in the Components folder, called ItemList.razor, in which you will copy the ArticleCategoryList code and define a parameter of type ItemListModel in place of the category array. Now, you need to edit the markup as in Listing 4-2 to create the table headers based on the ItemListModel headers, assuming that the collection is ordered based on the visualization preferences.

Listing 4-2. Extracting the List Component That Renders the Table Headers

```
<table>
  <thead>
    <tr>
      <th></th>
      @foreach (var header in Model.Headers)
```

```
    {
    <th>@header</th>
    }
    <th></th>
  </tr>
</thead>
```

Regarding the row, you can use .NET Reflection to inspect the object type and retrieve the properties, from which you can extract the values (Listing 4-3).

Listing 4-3. Extracting the List Component That Renders the Table Rows

```
<tbody>
 @foreach (var item in Model.Items)
 {
 <tr>
 <td><button class="btn btn-warning" @onclick="e =>
 OnEditClick.InvokeAsync(item)">Edit</button></td>
 @foreach(var property in item.GetType().GetProperties())
 {
 <td>@property.GetValue(item)</td>
 }
 <td><button class="btn btn-danger" @onclick="e =>
 ShowConfirm(item)">Delete</button></td>
 </tr>
 }
 </tbody>
</table>
```

In Chapter 3, I added the code to manage the user confirmation during the delete operation, by using the Bootstrap modal and taking advantage of the Blazor JavaScript interoperability functionality to open and close the modal with the jQuery functions. You can do the same in the component library: adding a JavaScript file in the wwwroot folder of the library and naming it, for example, frontendlib.js. You can copy the showConfirmDelete and hideConfirmDelete functions from the index.html file (the library compilation adds this file in the DLL). You can reference this file by appending the path _content/<DLL name>/<filename> in the index.html script. In this case, the reference is <script src="_content/frontendlib/frontendlib.js"> </script>.

This new component permits you to delete the article and article categories components on the front-end, and it allows you to create the list visualization for any entities of your application (Listing 4-4).

Listing 4-4. Extracting the ArticleCategories Page That Shows the Use of the New ItemList Component

```
@inherits ArticleCategoriesBase
@page "/articlecategories"
<h2>Article Categories</h2>
<div class="mt-3">
    @if(categoryModel.Item == null)
    {
        <ItemList
            Model="categoriesModel"
            OnAddClick="AddCategory"
            OnEditClick="EditCategory"
            OnDeleteClick="DeleteCategory">
        </ItemList>
    }
    else { ... }
</div>
```

Creating a Templated Component

There are a few occasions when using parameters can be too complex to generalize the content of a component. Moreover, you may need to show a piece of markup specified by the parent component to provide maximum flexibility for the user of your library. Blazor offers the ability to project markup into a component, creating parameters of RenderFragment type. Components that use parameters of RenderFragment type, are called templated components, allowing the use of one or more templates in them.

This ability is the perfect way to create a container component, where the specific markup is always the same. Check out the application details components called Article.razor and ArticleCategory.razor. Both of these components use different fields inside the EditForm, but DataAnnotationValidator, ValidationSummary, and the submit and cancel buttons are the same. You could create a model and use .NET Reflection to generate the fields like in the List component, but in my experience, the autogenerated details forms work fine for the user of the library only in simple cases. A templated component provides significant flexibility, and Blazor provides a simple way to implement them.

Let's create an ItemDetails.razor file in the Components folder of the components library and use the code in Listing 4-5. The parameter FieldsTemplate receives the markup that Blazor places at the @FieldTemplate position. You are not limited to one parameter of type RenderFragment, so you can make more parts of your component replaceable with custom markup using the father component.

Listing 4-5. Extracting the Details Component that uses a template definition

```
<EditForm Model="@Model.Item" OnValidSubmit="@(e =>
OnSaveClick.InvokeAsync(Model.Item))">
 <DataAnnotationsValidator />
 <ValidationSummary />
  @FieldsTemplate
 <button type="submit" class="btn btn-primary">Save</button>
 <button type="button" class="btn btn-warning"
 @onclick="OnCancelClick">Cancel</button>
</EditForm>

@code {
 [Parameter]
 public RenderFragment FieldsTemplate { get; set; }
 [Parameter]
 public ItemDetailsModel Model { get; set; }
  ...
}
```

In Listing 4-6, you can see how to use the component. Between the opening and closing ItemDetails tags, you can create a new element with the name of the parameter, in this case <FieldsTemplate>. You can put whatever you want in this parameter. Blazor projects the content of this element into the component ItemDetails. If you have more than one RenderFragment parameter, you can create more elements with the respective names in the ItemDetails elements.

Listing 4-6. Using the Details Component

```
<ItemDetails
  ItemType="ArticleCategoryItem"
  Model="categoryModel"
  OnSaveClick="SaveCategory"
  OnCancelClick="ShowList">
  <FieldsTemplate>
  <!-- place here your markup -->
  </FieldsTemplate>
</ItemDetails>
```

This is a fantastic feature that allows you to go more in-depth with the generalization of a component. But Blazor can do more.

Creating a Generic Component

If the content of a project needs to access some data of a component, you can use the generic version of RenderFragment and pass to it an instance of the generic type. In our case, we need to pass the model of the details form to the RenderFragment, so we create a specific type called ItemDetailsModel, and then we can use it as the generic type for the RenderFragment.

However, we cannot use the type Object for the item, like we did for the item array of the List component, because the binding of the form elements requires us to know the item fields. For example, if we have to bind the field Name of the Category with an InputText component, we must have access to the field, and an Object does not allow this. Moreover, in the component, we do not know that the object is a category because it must work with any entity of the project. The best way to solve this problem in the .NET Framework is to use a generic type in the definition, which means creating a generic ItemDetailsModel (Listing 4-7).

Listing 4-7. Defining the Generic Item Details Model

```
public class ItemDetailsModel<TItem>
{
  public string ItemName { get; set; }
  public TItem Item { get; set; }
}
```

We can, therefore, kill two birds with one stone and take advantage of another peculiar characteristic of the Blazor components: the generic components. Still, thanks to the @typeparam directive, we can create an ItemType and use it as a generic type everywhere in the component and then, in the ItemDetailsModel and RenderFragment too, obtain the maximum possible generalization (Listing 4-8).

Listing 4-8. Defining the Item Details Component with a Generic Type

```
@typeparam ItemType
<EditForm Model="@Model.Item" OnValidSubmit="@(e =>
OnSaveClick.InvokeAsync(Model.Item))">
 <DataAnnotationsValidator />
 <ValidationSummary />
  @FieldsTemplate(Model.Item)
 <button type="submit" class="btn btn-primary">Save</button>
 <button type="button" class="btn btn-warning"
 @onclick="OnCancelClick">Cancel</button>
</EditForm>

@code {
 [Parameter]
 public RenderFragment<ItemType> FieldsTemplate { get; set; }
 [Parameter]
 public ItemDetailsModel<ItemType> Model { get; set; }
  ...
}
```

When you use a generic component, you must specify the concrete type, using the name of the generic type name as a parameter. In this case, we called the generic type ItemType (@typeparam ItemType), so, for example, in the ArticleCategory component, we use the ItemDetails component with the ItemType parameter set to ArticleCategoryItem (Listing 4-9).

Listing 4-9. Using the Item Details Component in the ArticleCategories Page

```
<ItemDetails
 ItemType="ArticleCategoryItem"
 Model="categoryModel"
 OnSaveClick="SaveCategory"
 OnCancelClick="ShowList">
 <FieldsTemplate Context="Category">
 <div class="form-group">
 <label for="name">Name: </label>
 <InputText id="name" @bind-Value="Category.Name"
 class="form-control" />
 <ValidationMessage For="@(() => Category.Name)" />
 </div>
 <div class="form-group">
 <label for="description">Description: </label>
 <InputTextArea id="description" @bind-Value="Category.
 Description" class="form-control" />
 </div>
 </FieldsTemplate>
</ItemDetails>
```

We can access the RenderFragment context by specifying the
Context parameter, as shown in Listing 4-9, where we set the
Context of the FieldsTemplate to Category. So, the word Category
represents the instance of the item passed to the RenderFragment
(@FieldsTemplate(Model.Item)).

Using a specific context makes the code clearer, but it is not
mandatory: you could use the reserved word context. For example,
in Listing 4-9, you can omit Context="Category" and use @bind-
Value="context.Name" in the InputText component. In the code provided
with the book, I use both approaches as possible examples of use.

Creating Custom Input Components

Another good idea to simplify and make your code more maintainable is
to customize the collection of the input components. Taking a look at the
article category and article details forms, you will note that there is a lot of
repeated code, such as the bootstrap layout structure and the parameters
passed to the Blazor form components. If you need to change the layout or
the way you display a single field, you must change all this code. Using a
custom input component, you can create your UI components library and
reuse it in all your projects.

An input component inherits from the InputBase class, which accepts
a generic argument to specify the type of value managed. In many cases,
the value managed is a string, like for the InputText and InputTextArea.
In Listing 4-10, you can see the markup and the code to generalize the use
of an InputText. You can create a component named FieldInputText and
show the label for the input only if the user provides the value.

Listing 4-10. The Custom Input Text Component Definition

```
@inherits InputBase<string>
<div class="form-group">
 @if (!string.IsNullOrWhiteSpace(Label))
 {
 <label for="@Id">@Label: </label>
 }
 <InputText id="@Id" @bind-Value="@CurrentValue" class="form-
 control" />
 <ValidationMessage For="@Validation" />
</div>
@code
{
 [Parameter] public string Id { get; set; }
 [Parameter] public string Label { get; set; }
 [Parameter] public Expression<Func<string>> Validation { get;
 set; }

 protected override bool TryParseValueFromString(string value,
 out string result, out string validationErrorMessage)
 {
 result = value;
 validationErrorMessage = null;
 return true;
 }
}
```

The Input base abstract class requires us to implement the
TryParseValueFromString method because, in case our input manages
a value of a type different from the string, we must provide the correct
conversion from the string value. The current value is available in the
@CurrentValue property of the base class, which is the same type of the

generic for the class (in our case a string). You can do the same work for the InputTextArea and use it and the InputText component to simplify the article category page (Listing 4-11).

Listing 4-11. Using the Custom Input Components

```
<ItemDetails ...>
  <FieldsTemplate Context="Category">
    <FieldInputText
        Id="name" Label="Name"
        @bind-Value="Category.Name"
        Validation="@(() => Category.Name)" />
    <FieldInputTextArea
        Id="description" Label="Description"
        @bind-Value="Category.Description"
        Validation="@(() => Category.Description)" />
  </FieldsTemplate>
</ItemDetails>
```

If the value is always a string and the component parameters are always the same (Id, Label, and Validation), we can create a base class that inherits from the InputBase to collect the parameters and implement the conversion method. We can name this class FieldInputBase and use it to simplify the specific component code (Listing 4-12).

Listing 4-12. The Base Class Definition for the Custom Input Text Components

```
public abstract class FieldInputBase : InputBase<string>
{
  [Parameter] public string Id { get; set; }
  [Parameter] public string Label { get; set; }
  [Parameter] public Expression<Func<string>> Validation { get;
  set; }
```

```
protected override bool TryParseValueFromString(string value,
out string result, out string validationErrorMessage)
{
    result = value;
    validationErrorMessage = null;
    return true;
}
}
```

Thanks to this class, in many cases we only need to create the specific markup, as shown in Listing 4-13.

Listing 4-13. The Input Text Component Definition Simplified by the FieldInputBase Class

```
@inherits FieldInputBase
<div class="form-group">
 @if (!string.IsNullOrWhiteSpace(Label))
 {
 <label for="@Id">@Label: </label>
 }
 <InputTextArea id="@Id" @bind-Value="@CurrentValue"
 class="form-control" />
 <ValidationMessage For="@Validation" />
</div>
```

The Blazor form components have some limitations, like the ability to work with a string value only. Generally, this is not a problem, but sometimes it is required that you convert the current string to a specific value. This is the case of the InputSelect, where the value of the selection must be a string. We are using the InputSelect for the category of an article, and, to solve the problem, we used a string value on the front-end and converted it to an integer on the back-end.

With a custom component, you can also solve this problem thanks to the generic implementation of the base class InputBase. In Listing 4-12, we are using a string for the generic parameter, but we can require the generic type of each component, including the InputSelect (Listing 4-14).

Listing 4-14. The Generic Implementation of the FieldInputBase

```
public class FieldInputBase<T> : InputBase<T>
{
  ...
  protected override bool TryParseValueFromString(string value,
  out T result, out string validationErrorMessage)
  {
    Type paramType = typeof(T);
    switch (paramType.FullName)
    {
        case "System.String":
            result = (T)(object)value; break;
        case "System.Int32":
            result = (T)(object)int.Parse(value); break;
        default:
            throw new NotSupportedException($"FieldInputBase
            does not support the type {paramType}");
    }
    validationErrorMessage = null;
    return true;
  }
}
```

The code gets a little complicated because we need to use .NET Reflection to understand the current type and correctly convert the value in the TryParseValueFromString method. We used a switch to allow the addition of other cases, like Boolean, Guid, and enumeration.

With this change, your `FieldSelectInput` needs only an additional parameter for the selected items; the rest is handled by the base class (Listing 4-15).

Listing 4-15. The Field Select Component Implementation

```
@inherits FieldInputBase<int>
...
<InputSelect id="@Id" @bind-Value="@CurrentValueAsString"
class="form-control">
@foreach(var item in SelectItems)
{
<option value="@item.Value">@item.Label</option>
}
...
@code {
 [Parameter] public InputSelectItem[] SelectItems { get; set; }
}
```

Note that the `bind-Value` uses `CurrentValueAsString` (defined in the `InputBase` class) instead of `CurrentValue`: the `InputSelect` needs a string, not an integer. Without this change, Blazor treats the integer like a string, and all the internal comparisons when the value changes do not work.

Summary

Creating a library of components greatly simplifies the code of your project, allows you to divide the work between components, and reuse what you have done in other projects. However, it requires you to analyze the requirements to better generalize the components, without going overboard with generalization.

In this chapter, you saw how to use the power of the .NET Framework in a single-page application using .NET Reflection and the generic types. You can make something similar in JavaScript, supported by powerful tools like TypeScript, but in the .NET Framework you have a strict typing system that makes these techniques less prone to errors.

When starting your project, spend a lot of time to make your components reusable and collect them into a library. If you don't go overboard with generalizations, you will save a lot of time when maintaining your project by investing a little more in the beginning.

CHAPTER 5

Deploy Your Application

Your application is ready, so it is time to make it available to your users. The deployment process is different between Blazor Server and Blazor WebAssembly, and it also depends on the scalability that you would like your application to have.

The word *scalability* is a simple concept, but it is not simple to implement. Scalability refers to the ability of a system to keep its performance constant by dynamically increasing its available resources as the number of users increases. Scalability is a requirement in today's world; you must address it at the beginning of the development process, because it impacts how the application will be developed.

In this chapter, you will see some of the choices you have to deploy your application, and we will look at some considerations based on the typical requirements of a business application.

Deploying a Blazor Server App

A Blazor Server app is a .NET Core application that uses SignalR to keep the user interface up-to-date. We can prepare the package to be published from a terminal window, using the `dotnet publish -c Release` command of the .NET CLI. The CLI creates a `publish` folder with the build

© Michele Aponte 2020

M. Aponte, *Building Single Page Applications in .NET Core 3,*
https://doi.org/10.1007/978-1-4842-5747-0_5

artifact, but you can change this default folder using the -o option of the
dotnet publish command. If you use Visual Studio, you can use the Build
➤ Publish menu and select a target folder.

After the build operation, you have to deploy the package, and you
have to choose where to place the application. Any deployment option that
supports ASP.NET Core 3 is available for Blazor; the most commonly used
are IIS, an Azure web app, and a Docker image.

To use IIS, you need Windows 8 (or later) or Windows Server 2012 R2
(or later). To host the ASP.NET Core application, IIS needs the .NET Core
Hosting Bundle, which installs the .NET Core Runtime, the .NET Core
Library, and the ASP.NET Core Module.

The ASP.NET Core Module allows the use of .NET Core in IIS, but you
can decide how it must work by choosing between two hosting models:
in-process and out-of-process. All the HTTP requests to your application
are handled by the w3wp.exe process and passed to the ASP.NET Core
Module. If you choose the in-process models, the ASP.NET Core Module
passes the request to your code, creating the HttpContext and using the
same IIS worker process. If you choose the out-of-process hosting models,
your code runs in a separate process, so the ASP.NET Core Module needs
to forward the HTTP request to Kestrel (Figure 5-1).

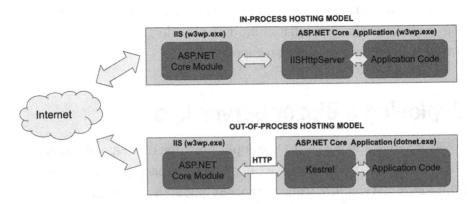

Figure 5-1. *ASP.NET Core in-process and out-of-process hosting
models*

The in-process hosting model is more efficient and should be your first choice (this is why it is the default hosting model). Use out-of-process only for deployment compatibility reasons.

Blazor Server uses SignalR, so you need to support it. To improve the performance of the application, you have to reduce the latency between the client and the server. To do that, adding WebSocket support is the best choice. When you use IIS, support for WebSocket is already enabled, so if the application forces the use of the long polling, you must check the configuration.

If you need to scale the application instances to support more users, you have to configure your cluster to ensure that all requests are received by the same node that starts the SignalR communication. On-premises, you can do this using sticky sessions (better known as *session affinity* by some load balancers).

If you use Microsoft Azure, you can deploy your Blazor Server application to an Azure Web App, the most popular Azure service that provides you with scalable hosting that supports both Windows and Linux. It is part of the platform as a service (PaaS) offered by Microsoft and allows you to create and manage a web application from the Azure Portal and use the integrated tools for Visual Studio and Visual Studio Code.

You can try this service by signing up for an Azure account for free. From the Azure Portal, you can create a new web app, configuring the few requested fields (Figure 5-2).

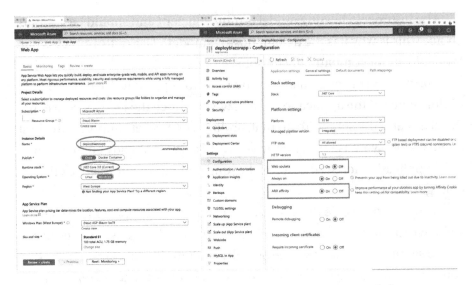

Figure 5-2. *The creation panel of an Azure web app and the configuration for a Blazor Server application*

The WebSocket support is set to false by default, so you need to go to the Configuration ➤ General settings and turn on the "Web sockets" option. In this panel, you can also see the "ARR affinity" option, already turned on, that allows sticky sessions when you request the web app to manually or automatically scale the nodes of the cluster.

You can deploy a Blazor Server app to an Azure web app with different automation tools, but to simplify the process, you can use the Publish menu of Visual Studio to start a step-by-step wizard (Figure 5-3).

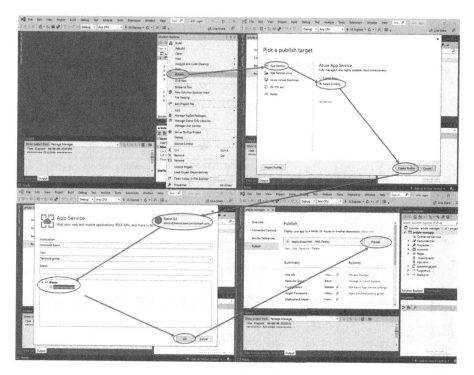

Figure 5-3. *Visual Studio 2019 deploy wizard for an existing Azure web app*

I prefer Visual Studio Code, which provides a fantastic plug-in to manage Azure services: right-click the Publish folder, choose the target Web App, and confirm the deploy (Figure 5-4).

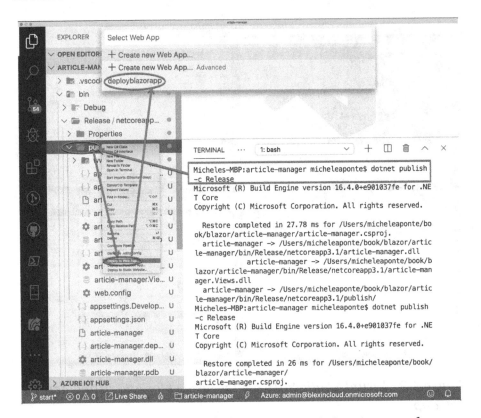

Figure 5-4. *Deploying an application to an existing Azure web app from Visual Studio Code*

If you have a large number of users, Azure provides you with a separate service called Azure SignalR Service to manage SignalR connections. All .NET Core applications support the integration of this service and therefore Blazor Server application. Check the official documentation for the configuration steps (`https://docs.microsoft.com/en-US/aspnet/core/host-and-deploy/blazor/server?view=aspnetcore-3.1`).

Deploying a Blazor WebAssembly App

Performing a build of a Blazor WebAssembly app produces static files that the browser downloads and executes. These files can be developed anywhere that you can make them available for download via HTTP protocol; then, you can choose to expose them standalone by any web server you want. For example, you can use IIS, Azure Web App, Azure Storage (which allows you to configure a BLOB container as a static web site hosting space), Nginx (with Docker or not), and even GitHub Pages.

The command to build a Blazor WebAssembly app is the same as a Blazor Server: `dotnet publish -c Release`. The `bin/Release/ netstandard2.1/publish` folder contains a folder with the name of the project and a subfolder called `dist`, which includes the static files that you can deploy, for example, to BLOB storage configured as a static web site (Figure 5-5).

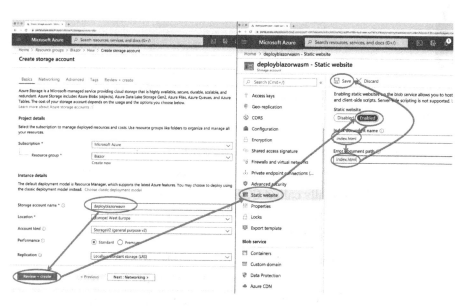

Figure 5-5. *Configuration of a static web site with Azure Storage*

This static web site is a BLOB named $web where you can upload the files of the dist folder; you can do this via the Azure Portal or the Microsoft Azure Storage Explorer, a free tool to manage Azure Storage accounts (Figure 5-6).

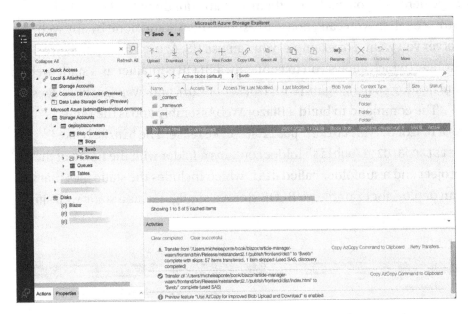

Figure 5-6. *Blazor WebAssembly app uploaded with Azure Storage Explorer*

This operation deploys only the front-end, so if you have a back-end, you need to deploy it and allow calls from the domain of the front-end (technically called CORS policies; you can read more here: https://docs.microsoft.com/en-US/aspnet/core/security/cors?view=aspnetcore-3.1).

Another possibility is to serve the front-end with an ASP.NET Core application, using ASP.NET Core hosting. Which is the best way for your app depends on the scalability and security requirements you have. If your application structure includes an ASP.NET Core back-end that exposes REST APIs and a front-end that is a Blazor WebAssembly app, you can deploy them in the same project, copying the `dist` folder of the Blazor project into the `wwwroot` folder on the ASP.NET Core API project. In this case, the domains of the API and the front-end are the same, so you do not need to configure CORS policies. The negative aspect is that you must scale both the back-end and the front-end if you need to scale your application to manage more users. If the front-end does not change, the users do not download it again, but the front-end continues to call the APIs during application usage. You could probably scale only the back-end if you separated it from the front-end. The same problem occurs if you need to update the user interface without any impact on the back-end: if you separate the two layers, you can scale only the front-end for a short period to allow all the clients to download the new versions.

Summary

With the deployment of a Blazor application, our journey to create single-page applications with Blazor has come to an end. As you saw in this chapter, the deployment scenarios are different depending on whether you use Blazor Server or Blazor WebAssembly. But more important are the requirements you have: based on them, you can choose how to distribute your application, which inevitably, in the simplest cases, consists of both a front-end layer and a back-end layer. The complexity of deployment often increases with the scalability that you want to achieve, but there may also be security requirements that can lead you to different choices. Never underestimate them.

Except for some advanced aspects, such as content protection or optimization tips provided by the framework, you now have all the necessary knowledge to develop your business application with .NET Core. As always, practice is your best teacher!

Index

© Michele Aponte 2020
M. Aponte, *Building Single Page Applications in .NET Core 3,*
https://doi.org/10.1007/978-1-4842-5747-0

Printed in the United States
By Bookmasters